Endless Miracles

from your friend

Endless
Miracles

by
Jack Ratz

Introduction by
Howard L. Adelson

Shengold Publishers, Inc.

ISBN: 0-88400-202-0
Library of Congress Catalog Card Number: 97-062062

Published by Shengold Publishers, Inc.

First Edition 1998
Second Printing 1999
Third Printing 2000
Fourth Printing 2001
Fifth Printing 2003
Sixth Printing 2004
Seventh Printing 2005

This book is dedicated to the Latvian victims of the Holocaust, especially my family: my mother, brothers, grandparents, uncles, aunts and cousins, who were killed in 1941 only because they were Jews.

I also dedicate this book to the suffering and torture endured by the small number of survivors of Latvian Jewry, including my father, may he rest in peace, and my cousin Max, who remains in Riga to this day, and the other Latvian survivors who are spread throughout the world.

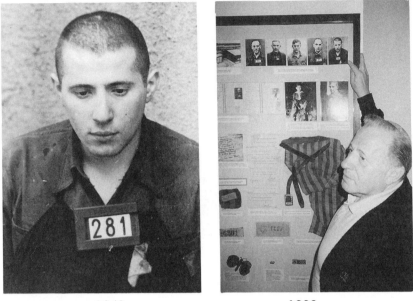

1942   1998

As I mentioned in the book, I have gone back to visit Riga many times and on my last visit, I had a most remarkable experience. In the city's Holocaust museum, during the course of a tour, our guide pointed out a row of photographs of young men from Riga, some mere teenagers, who had perished in the Shoah. I was completely taken aback when I noticed that the last photograph in the row was of me!

CONTENTS

PREFACE

As I prepare this book for the fourth edition, I feel that, in addition to sharing my wartime experiences, I would like to share with you the incredible events that have occurred in the four years since the first edition went to press in 1998. So-called historians have tried to deny the horrifying crimes that were perpetrated against the Jewish people during the Second World War. I, and the thousands who managed to survive the Holocaust, saw, with our own eyes, how entire Jewish communities — men, women, and children — were simply eradicated, in most unthinkable ways, not only in the ghettos, but in concentration camps, labor camps, and death camps.

Our testimony is sufficient to put the lie to the revisionists who deny the Holocaust, but if other proof is needed, it is to be found in the headlines of our daily newspapers. Very simply, if the Holocaust is not an historic fact, would the German government attempt to compensate the handful of survivors with monetary restitution? I, as well as many of the others who succeeded in surviving the Holocaust, am trying to explain the events of the past and to teach youngsters the truth about this almost unbelievable chapter of history.

In the years since the first publication of this book, I have responded to quite a number of congregations and many schools — including numerous public schools — which invited me to talk to them. Most interesting to me are the questions that the children ask, and subsequently, the flood of letters I have received from middle and high school students and staff. I could fill another volume with these missives, which are remarkable for their empathy and appreciation.

The attention and full concentration of my listeners proves to me the importance of speaking to and teaching both adults and youngsters. Indeed, I hope that by publicizing the unimaginable facts, we will be able to avoid the repetition of the catastrophic events that transpired in Europe in the 1940s.

I sincerely hope that the impact of these teachings will achieve the results for which we are striving.

Professor S. Dubnow was shot in Rumbuli Forest on December 8, 1941. His final words expressed the hope that someone would remain alive and remember to write about the fate of the Latvian Jews. Hitler and his henchmen ensured that only .01% of Latvian Jews survived the Holocaust. I feel privileged to write this book to bear witness to the tragedy of the Holocaust, and as a symbol of hope in the future, which Hider could not destroy.

I write of my experience in the two ghettos, four work camps, concentration camp and displaced persons camp. I call the time I spent in the ghetto "the death dance," because we danced to our deaths. The camps were "death," the places where we were forced to die through hunger and hard labor. We were forced to sleep on wooden boards and the Nazis tormented us until we died.

I would like to bring out a lesson from the Hell we endured, to show how human beings behaved inhumanly. I know that anyone who suffered and lived through the war will never forget. We must make sure that the bitter lesson will be well learned, that history will not be permitted to repeat itself, and that the generations to come will never be forced to endure experiences like ours.

I would like to thank my *aishes chayil,* my devoted wife Doris, my children and the future, represented by my ten grandchildren for inspiring me and giving me the courage to write this living testament. I pray they will carry on the legacy of the murdered Latvian Jews.

ACKNOWLEDGMENTS

Heartfelt thanks to Felice Eisner. My appreciation cannot be adequately expressed to her for her dedication and devotion, which made a true labor of love of this work. Her tireless efforts created order from chaos and enabled me to achieve my goal of "telling the story."

To Moshe Sheinbaum, the publisher of this volume, for his wise counsel and guidance, and for his valuable comments, my cordial thanks.

I am most grateful to Professors Howard L. Adelson and Gertrude Schneider for the wealth of information that they shared with me.

INTRODUCTION

by Professor Howard L. Adelson
The City University of New York

There is no such individual as an "ordinary man," but even if there was, by no stretch of the imagination could Jack Ratz be included in that category. He would never be classified as being simply ordinary. The fact that he led an extraordinary life and emerged in his golden years as a man of enormous initiative, originality, pragmatic success, and above all of a thoroughly admirable moral character which bespeaks a strength of personality far exceeding what we would expect even from extraordinary men. To endure the unendurable and to retain his moral character in the face of all of the obstacles is a feat in itself. To succeed in life despite insuperable difficulties and suffering is a virtual miracle.

Jack Ratz was born into comfortable circumstances in what was then the Republic of Latvia. Like most Latvian Jews he felt himself to be secure as a child of barely thirteen in the warmth of a loving, religious family that would suddenly be caught up in the turmoil of Europe under first Soviet and then Nazi domination. The peaceful, if somewhat unpleasantly anti-Semitic, atmosphere of the Latvian Republic became a boiling cauldron on June 17, 1940, when Russian troops crossed the border and occupied the country. By that event the society and structure of

Latvia were torn apart and all sorts of criminal behavior was transformed into the norm. The Ratz family felt the full brunt of the communist invasion since they were the owners of a tailoring business, but because the family was not exiled to the depths of the Soviet Union, it was destined to experience the most hideous fate that could befall a Jewish family in modern times, the Holocaust. When Germany invaded the Soviet Union on June 22, 1941, the worst destiny was visited upon the unfortunate Jews who were caught in the machinery of evil. Young people in the United States, and, indeed, some of the older ones as well, cannot fathom the depth of the tragedy that ensued because they cannot conceive of a world in which the goal of the government of society was the destruction of the Jewry. For the Nazis, Jewish survival in any form, even the most innocuous, was unendurable.

The Holocaust has led many Jews to deny God and to struggle to comprehend the history of our own time in purely secular terms. Only those with enormous moral strength of character were able to endure the suffering and the constant fear that afflicted European Jewry during the Holocaust. In a quiet way, throughout the awful experience, Jack Ratz preserved that which was most precious, and insofar as that was possible, he assisted others to survive. Those who lacked that strength of character were among the first to yield to the oppressors or to perish. As one of the handful of survivors of the holocaust in Latvia—and they were only a bare few hundred from the many thousands of Latvian Jews who lived throughout the country, but particularly in the capital, Riga, before the arrival of the Nazi murderers—Jack Ratz has continued to this very moment to maintain his strength of character, sensitivity and devotion to Jewish morality and belief, as well as a most unusual willingness to assist others who have been less fortunate. He expresses in his life and in his altruism the highest ideals of Judaism.

In this account of his life, Jack Ratz does more than to describe the tragedies that surrounded him and the suffering that engulfed him during those awful years when it was, in effect, illegal and improper for a Jew to survive in the charnel house of Nazi Europe. It would have been sufficient for most readers to hear the tale of unbelievable suffering that continued year after year with increasing intensity, but Jack Ratz has turned his story into a glorious message of overcoming the gloomy past by detailing his visit to Riga and Israel for a month in 1988 and explaining what it means to have moments of joy in a Jewish family.

The visits to the scenes of the outrage, murder and suffering are particularly moving. He tells, without being gruesome or maudlin, of the murder of thousands upon thousands of innocent human beings solely because they were Jewish. He tells of how the few survivors of Latvian Jewry struggled to reconstruct their lives in the new environment of their native country while the Jews from other lands brought into the ghetto were either less able to survive the torment or were given privileged positions that might be denied to the Latvian Jews. Whereas most biographies about survivors, or autobiographies by those who endured the holocaust, end with the moment of liberation, as though that was truly the end of the story, Jack Ratz brings the story down to the present to explain how he conquered the effects of the great tragedy. The experience of the trauma was so deep that it became impossible for many of the survivors to revisit the scenes of the torture and suffering. Many simply placed the blame for their survival upon themselves, and they lost faith in any higher power. To others it became a horror that merely awoke the memories of the tragedies that they had witnessed and endured. Jack Ratz and his American family, however, turned that awful experience into a victorious commemoration of those who perished and a rededication of the survivors to the struggle to live for the good of others. At site after site, Jack Ratz reawakened the memory of those who perished, and because he had the enormous strength of religious conviction he was able to pray at every site to commemorate those who perished and to visit with those who survived with him. At every turn he mustered his own resources and those of his friends to give aid to the aging survivors and to restore the memory of those who paid the full measure in the persecution. He proclaimed in the most concrete fashion the victory that he had won over the oppressor by building a loving family that was a credit to all Jewry and by extending his helping hand to comfort and to assist others who were less fortunate.

It is in the survival and continuity of the Jewish tradition within his family that Jack Ratz has won his greatest victory over the oppressor who wanted to eradicate the Jewish people and Judaism. It was a supreme demonstration of an inflexible will that made it possible for Jack Ratz, who was very young at the time, to survive the horror and to assist his father and others to survive. When reading this book there is a tendency to forget just how young the author really was at the time. He had to behave with the wisdom and courage of an adult, if he was to survive and to help his father and others to do so as well. It was an even greater demonstration of human will power to retain the Judaism which had been the object of such hatred on the part of the oppressors. Jack Ratz possesses that sense of History that permits him to view his own experience not merely as a participant in this cruel tragedy but as one who can analyze with a clear mind the vulgarity of the persecutors.

This is a book which does not spare the oppressors, nor does it concentrate on other individuals who were players in the tragedy. At one point he describes an ss Officer, Fritz Scherwitz, who was, in fact, a Jew who had been taken to Germany by a German soldier in the turmoil after the First World War. It was his fortune to become an ss officer who was sent to command the Lenta labor camp. Obviously he had to conceal from all the fact that he was Jewish, but he actually did everything possible at Lenta, even at the greatest risk to himself, to save some Jews. Nevertheless, it is sad to relate that he suffered denazification and imprisonment after the Second World War and was eventually lost to the Jewish people.

Jack Ratz details the worst features of the suffering in the ghettos, labor camps, extermination camps, forced marches and transport by sea. Throughout, the story is punctuated by murders and cruelty. He demonstrates repeatedly that only a hair's breadth separated life from death in the years from 1941 through 1945. The dangers did not end even with liberation, and many were lost, or lost the faith of survival, in that tragic period as well. Nevertheless the process of reconstructing life and escaping the grip of the Russian army, moving out of the displaced persons camps in the western zone and setting roots for a new life in freedom was very difficult. Many failed to achieve that goal.

In his new life, Jack Ratz not only raised and educated his own fine family, but he also devoted himself to educating other youth in the significance of the holocaust. Speaking in schools, writing about the horror of his stolen youth and showing by example that an individual can rise above the greatest of tragedies to recover a meaningful life, is an accomplishment in itself. Jack Ratz has given the reader much to ponder. He has a story that covers a half century that mirrors the contest between good and evil. It is the confrontation with evil while retaining the drive to do good that is at the root of this tale. He tells of the tragedies that surrounded the persecuted and the miracles of salvation that allowed some to live. There is a full exposition of the terror and the tension which reduced many to hopelessness and consequent failure. Above all, however, it is the story of success and perseverance that shine through the unbelievable dangers and obstacles which is important.

Family group, ca. 1910. My mother is the girl wearing the white dress in the front row. Directly behind her is her mother.

1

RIGA

I WAS BORN IN 1927 in Riga, Latvia, the son of a Jewish tailor.
My first terrible memory occurred when I was not quite thirteen. It was the morning of June 17, 1940. I awoke as usual,
dressed, and went to school with my books. In school someone
yelled that the Russian army had invaded Latvia and was
already in Riga.

This was appalling news. After centuries of oppression by
alternating German and Russian conquerors, Latvia in 1918
had become a self-governing republic and had maintained its
independence ever since. Indeed, on August 11, 1920, the
Soviet government had signed a treaty renouncing all authority
over Latvia and Latvians. And now . . .

I left my books in school and ran to see if it was true that the
Russians were in our city. I arrived in the middle of the city
near the railroad station and there, sure enough, was a huge
Russian tank with soldiers in it.

Some of the passersby were happy but others were deeply
upset that the Russians had invaded their country, an act of
treachery. They cursed and pounded on the side of the tank.
There were arguments and screams; then suddenly the tank
began to move.

I gaped in horror as it ran over some people, leaving their crushed and bloody bodies in the street.

That was the first time in my life that I saw bloodshed and corpses. I had never seen anything so ghastly and couldn't wait to tell my parents. I couldn't control myself and ran home in shock.

I have never forgotten that unspeakable scene. It's still in front of my eyes to this day. Yes, it still is. To see something like that, to experience such a sight, at that stage in my young life, was to burn horror into my memory. But in time worse was to come.

My three younger brothers, eleven, nine and one-month-old, were waiting at home. My older brother, Mendel, sixteen-and-a-half, was at work. My mother tried to calm me down as I poured out the story of the horrors I had seen. But I could tell that she too was shaken by what I reported.

The next day I went to school, but I could not wipe away what had happened the day before. After school, some friends and I decided to go and take another look at the tanks at the railway station. People were demonstrating both for and against the Russian army. Again there was bloodshed. People started fighting in the streets. It was chaos again, and again I ran home.

The demonstrations went on for a few days, until some people were arrested and the Russian government officially stepped in to control Latvia. They had always lusted after it.

Latvia, one of the Baltic States, has been a pivotal country historically, due to its prime location on the Baltic Sea. With a perfect natural harbor at Riga, it has always been a center of commerce and migration. Jews have lived in Riga at least since 1536, when a sales receipt was recorded between a Jew and a merchant in Riga.

Most Jews were prohibited from living in Riga by the order of the German burghers, who ruled Riga in the sixteenth century and considered Jews undesirable aliens. For hundreds of years, Jews had no right of residence and the few who lived in Latvia did so illicitly. In 1903, Russia offered to include Riga in the Pale of Settlement, a belt of territory in westernmost Russia, extending from the Baltic to the Black Sea. This offer gave Jews the right to live in Riga, but the German population there protested, so Riga remained "outside the Pale."

An exception was permitted my family because of my maternal grandfather, Aharon David Schusterman. In 1870, he was caught by "recruiters" and impressed into the tsar's army, where he served for twenty-five years. In 1895 his long years of service earned him—and by extension his family—the right of residence in Riga, because of the exceptions that were made for retired soldiers and various select others, and he lived there for the rest of his life, and my mother and the rest of us after him.

In 1842, only 409 Jews were registered as residents of Riga; however, by 1913, restrictions had been eased and more than 33,000 Jews were listed. November 18, 1918 was an important date for all Latvians, because that was the date that an independent provisional government was first set up. November 18 was the "Fourth of July" for Latvians, and I remember celebrating it as a holiday. We used to go the palace, the government headquarters in downtown Riga, and watch the parade. The streets were lined with firepots right up to the palace gates, and we would wait eagerly for President Carl Ulmanis to make a speech in honor of the occasion. Those were the good old days for us as children in Riga.

Before World War II, under the rule of the independent Latvian republic (1918–1940), Jews were accepted as members of society, and formed many organizations and welfare societies.

Riga was home to numerous branches of Judaism, ranging from Hasidic to secularist. Zionism was represented early on; in the 1880s, *Hovevei Zion* (Lovers of Zion) groups were formed in cities throughout Latvia, including Riga. The First Conference of the *Hovevei Zion*, which was held in Kattowitz (now Katowicz,

Poland) in 1884, had two delegates from Latvia. This year is the 100th anniversary of the First Zionist Congress in 1897, where two of the delegates, Leib Shalit of Riga and S. Zaks of Daugavpils, represented Latvian Jews.

My own school, Torah v'Derech Eretz, was fervently Jewish. We spoke Hebrew in and out of class, whenever we were on school grounds, even during recess and sports.

Latvia's Jews from various sects were world-famous. The noted Rabbi, Mordechai Nurok, represented Latvian Jews at the Second Conference of Russian Zionists in 1902. He served as a member of the Latvian Parliament and was a prominent leader of world Jewry. The influence of world Jewish organiza-

tions was instrumental in obtaining his release from the Soviet Union in 1945, and he later emigrated to Israel. He was a National Religious Party Member of the Knesset, a member of the government, and a candidate for president of Israel.

Latvian Jews had an impact on the State of Israel even in the pre-Zionist days, founding communities and establishing commercial and industrial enterprises. Many Latvian Jews became outstanding figures in Israel,

Rabbi Mordechai Nurok

in such varied fields as politics, the judiciary, education, publishing, and medicine.

Groups of Latvian Jews made *aliyah* in the pre-State days, before Herzl's Zionism, as part of the Yishuv. In 1891, they founded Hedera under severe conditions, while in 1901 settlers from Daugavpils, members of *Zeirei Zion*, established homes in Palestine.

The renowned Rabbi Abraham Isaac Kook, a Jew from Bausk in the south of Latvia, made *aliyah* to Jaffa (Yafo) in 1904,

Rabbi Abraham Isaac Kook

and served as the chief rabbi of Israel from 1919 until his death in 1935.

Dr. Jacob Hellman was a scholar and journalist who, as an ardent Zionist, led the Labor Wing of the Zionist movement and had a strong impact on the development of Jewish life. He was a representative of the World Jewish Congress, and spent many years in Argentina, an important figure in South American Jewry.

Zionism had a strong hold on many Latvian Jews, but other elements of Judaism were also vibrantly alive in Latvia. Riga

Rabbi Mordechai Dubin

was "the cradle of the Revisionist movement," headed by Dr. Jacob Hoffman. The Revisionist Movement was a revolt within the socialist parties against strict Marxian ideology. Zeev Jabotinsky's lecture in Russian brought about the formation of an offshoot of the world Revisionist movement.

The "Bund," too, was strong, with a representative in the Latvian Parliament, Dr. Noah Maisel. The Bund helped many Jewish organizations, schools, and cultural institutions, but fought against Zionism and the Hebrew education system. Dr. Maisel was deported to the Gulag by the Soviets in 1941, and died there.

Other anti-Zionist groups included the National Democratic Party and the Agudat Israel, led by Rabbi Mordechai Dubin and Shimon Wittenburg, members of Parliament. Rabbi Dubin was always ready to help people, no matter what their affiliation, and had close contacts in government circles. His influence was due to his warmth and care for individual Jews who needed his help, to whom his door was always open. He too was arrested in 1941 and deported to the Gulag, where he died.

Simon Dubnow, the famous Jewish historian, who wrote a ten-volume children's history of the Jews in Yiddish, *Das Yiddische Geschichte, derzeilt far Kinder*, lived in Riga from 1933. In 1941, the Gestapo arrested him and sent his library and archives to Germany.

Professor Dubnow was sent to the large ghetto, and killed in the mass executions on December 8, 1941, along with my mother and brothers. He continued to write even in the ghetto, and his last words were *"Schreibt, Yidden, schreibt* (Write, Jews, write)."* I took Professor Dubnow's words to heart, and he is part of the inspiration for this book. The tortures that the Germans inflicted on us must be recorded and heeded by the world.

Professor Simon Dubnow

Great rabbis held rabbinical positions throughout Latvia, including the rabbis of the Don Yahia family, who had come to Lutzin from Spain and Portugal. Rabbi Zack, chief rabbi of Riga, a great Torah scholar, was also killed by the Nazis. Rabbi Joseph Isaac Schneurson of Lubavitch also lived in Riga before emigrating to the United States, and left behind a legacy of Habad Hasidism.

Among the rabbis of Latvia are two most outstanding rabbinical authorities, both of Daugavpils. Rabbi Meir Simcha HaCohen was the author of *Or Someach* (Joyous Light) and Rabbi Joseph Rosen, known as the Rogachever Rov, wrote *Tsafenat Paneach* (Interpreter of Secrets). Rabbi Meir Simcha was the head of the Mitnagdim, the anti-Hasidic groups, while Rabbi Rosen led the chasidim. Each of them led his respective congregation for over fifty years. The impact of their scholarship between the two world wars was felt by the Jewish people everywhere.

The Rogachever Gaon won the respect of all with his brilliant mind and outstanding scholarship. He knew the entire Torah and Talmudic reference works by heart. Even Rabbi HaCohen

Rabbi Joseph Rosen, the Rogachever Gaon

credited the superiority of his scholarship; the story is told that once Rabbi HaCohen was presented with a very difficult problem; he admitted that he would have to struggle all night to find a solution, then added, "But step in to the Rogachever and he will answer you on the spot."

The last rabbi from Riga died in 1957. Rabbi Moshe David Masliansky had been rabbi in Valk, Estonia, before World War II. He had studied in the Volozhin Yeshiva with the Gaon, and said that even before his Bar Mitzvah, he was known as the most outstanding of all the students. The head of the yeshiva did not confer rabbinical authorization on him, saying that he was acceptable without it.

O. O. Gruzenberg, the outstanding lawyer, lived in Riga for several years and took an active part in Jewish community life. He defended Mendel Beiliss in the infamous Russian Blood Libel case in 1911–13, when the fate of Russia's Jewry hung in the balance, when a guilty verdict would have resulted in a bloody pogrom. (Not that the tsarists ever needed an excuse.)

Rabbi Meir Simcha HaCohen

In short, Riga's Jews were active in education, the arts, the theater, medicine, law, professional life, and business, including export-import. The Jews were involved in the stock market and founded a Shomer Shabbat bank for Riga's Jews.

The lady who became my grandmother, Chava Riva Zahl, was a widow with four children. She was interested in my grandfather and managed to disperse her children among friends and relatives long enough for my grandfather to propose marriage, unaware that she already had children. After the wedding she brought them home one by one. Later my Uncle Mendel was born in 1898 and my mother Tema in 1899.

Between 1895 and 1914, my bubby sent away most of the children of her first marriage. My uncle, her first son, Nathan Zahl, arrived in the United States in 1904. He married soon after; his daughter Jean was born in 1906. Bubby's daughter, my Aunt Fanny, came to America in 1914, while her brother remained in Russia in Yekatrinoslav (now Dnepropetrovsk in the Ukraine) and married there. The youngest daughter, Devorah, later called Vera, was put into an orphanage, married a non-Jew, and converted to Christianity. I still remember her. When her husband died she visited us in Riga, bringing with her a Mexican Chihuahua and a box of chocolates.

My grandparents remained in Riga with my mother. Her brother, my Uncle Mendel, was killed in 1917 because he was Jewish. The war was among the Bolsheviks, Germans, Poles and Latvians, but it was the Jews who suffered, as usual.

When my mother was twenty-one, my grandmother decided it was time to find a husband for her. Although my grandparents were poor, she wanted Tema to make a good match, and with her usual cunning, she made careful plans and preparations. My grandfather was a shoemaker, barely eking out a living, while the prospective *mechutan* (in-law), Reb Chaim Racs, was a wealthy man by the standards of his village, Barafka. Reb Chaim had built homes for all his children and one of his sons

My mother, Tema Schusterman,
before her marriage

had a general store on the large village square. When Reb Chaim arrived to meet the Schustermans, the shop was filled with numerous pairs of shoes. He was duly impressed and agreed to the match. Reb Chaim was thrilled that his son Moshe had the chance to marry into a rich businessman's family. In addition, through this marriage, Moshe would obtain the right to live in Riga and would be able to bring the rest of his own family to live in the metropolis.

After the wedding, Reb Chaim again went to visit the Schustermans. He came into the store where my grandmother, Chava Riva, sat, and began chatting with her. Suddenly, a neighboring merchant walked in and asked for several pairs of shoes. He took the shoes and left without paying. My grandfather was surprised, but didn't comment. Soon, however, he saw several other merchants come in, claim shoes, and leave. Finally, little by little, all the shoes were gone, and the store was empty.

My grandmother, Chava Riva, laughed and said, "I knew this would happen sooner or later, so it's just as well it happened now. We don't have a shoe store, just a shoe repair business. I borrowed shoes from all my neighbors to impress you. My husband, Aharon David, sits in the window at No. 2 Puskiniela and repairs shoes. I knew that if you, Reb Chaim, would know that your daughter-in-law had a cobbler for a father, you would never agree to the match. I had to improvise a scheme so that

My parents shortly after their marriage

my daughter could marry into a rich family so that she will have a better life in the future."

Reb Chaim smiled as he heard what Chava Riva said, and replied, "It's a pleasure to do business with you!"

My parents were married in Riga in 1922, and my brother Mendel was born on December 22, 1923. He was drafted into the Russian army and killed by the Germans in June 1942. Like my Uncle Mendel, my brother Mendel was only nineteen years old when he was killed.

I learned some of the details of my brother's death after many years. I began my search for him in July 1941, when the Germans brought hundreds of thousands of prisoners into Riga from various fronts. My parents had asked me to keep my eyes open and, if possible without danger to myself, try to find Mendel, who had disappeared one day, never returning from work. I looked for Mendel among the prisoners of war in Riga every day until we were locked up in the ghetto, to no avail.

After our liberation I searched for Mendel in Germany, Poland, and Russia. Whenever I met any former Russian soldiers, I asked them if they had known my brother. I asked anyone I met who had come from Riga if they knew what had happened to Mendel. Finally I heard from a friend of mine that he knew someone who had fought beside my brother in the Latvian Battalion against the German army. This man, Edel Kastres, had survived and lived in Haifa.

In 1969, I took my family to tour Israel, but made a side trip to see Mr. Kastres, leaving my wife and children to continue with our tour itinerary. I remembered Edel from before the war; he had been in our home many times. He described how my brother had been killed. Mendel had been wounded and was hospitalized when the news came that the Germans had killed all the Jews in Riga. Although he was far from recovered, he decided to return to the front to kill as many Germans as possible in revenge for the Jews of Riga, including our family. During the battle, he was shot in the head and killed instantly.

Yes, my long search was finally over, but the result was not what I had longed for. I rejoined my family on the tour with a broken heart. My daughter said, "Daddy, what happened?" At sixteen, she saw that something was wrong and was able to understand my feelings. Now I could rest from my search, but now I knew for certain that all my family had perished in the war. I had always cherished a forlorn hope that at least one brother had survived besides me, but now that hope was gone.

I didn't give up my hopes for the future, however. I made up my mind to enjoy my postwar family, my children and grand-children. God was good to me; He let my dream come true. I am a rich man with three married children and beautiful grandchildren; my wife and I are happy together, and we hope to see much pleasure and *nachas* from our family, as my parents did before the tragedies of the war.

2

CHILDHOOD

I REMEMBER THE GOOD LIFE we had when I was a child. We were five brothers. My older brother Mendel was born December 22, 1923, I was born December 26, 1927. My younger brothers were born February 28, 1930, and August 13,1931; the baby was born after the Russians took control of Latvia in 1940.

We went to school during the year and spent the summers in the country. Once I was sent to summer camp near the Baltic Sea. We went to shul on Shabbat and all the holidays.

My father had a tailor shop where he oversaw several employees. The shop was in our home; we had a large apartment. We had electricity, a radio and a telephone. When I got older, I had a bicycle.

When I was not quite three, my maternal grandmother died. We lived at No. 2 Pushkiniela, with my grandfather's shoe repair shop in the front ground floor apartment. At that time, three of us brothers were already born; I was the middle son. My mother took only me to the cemetery; I suppose the baby was too young and Mendel may have been in school. I still remember the funeral. Soon after, we moved from Puskiniela.*

---

* The sufix *-iela* means "street." Pushkiniela is "Pushkin Street."

My grandfather went to live in an old age home, where he died in 1934.

The Wall Street stock market crash of 1929 had caused repercussions all over the world, and we were in the middle of a depression. I was too young to understand at that time, but when I got older, I realized that we too had been affected by the Great Depression. People had no work and no money, and my mother was pregnant again. A friend took us in to live in the attic of his home on Jesusbashitzsiela. We lived there for a few months until my younger brother was born. He was named after my grandmother, Chava Riva; my parents called him Chona Rueven, and he brought us luck.

My father found work and a new apartment at No. 6 Jesusbashitzsiela. It was an eight-family house across from a club that catered wedding parties and had a tremendous yard in the front. The entrance to our building was at the back, with four apartments upstairs and four downstairs. There was a communal outhouse in the hall and a communal garbage bin in the backyard. Every few weeks, men would come at night with a horse-drawn wagon to take away the garbage and the sewage.

Our apartment was spacious and roomy. The hallway held a big closet where my mother kept the Passover dishes and stored the rendered fat we used at Seder. We lived there for about seven years. I spent my early childhood in this house. We boys had plenty of friends and played many games, including "tickets" and *skach ki*. At that time there were three railroad stations in Riga. One took people west to the Baltic Sea, one east toward Russia, and the third south toward France. Travelers handed in their tickets to the conductor, and he saved them for us children. He didn't give us the tickets until we paid a penalty—he insisted that we smell chloroform. The powerful odor caused us to cough violently, after which he gave us the tickets. Local tickets were worth less than long-distance tickets, and we used to trade back and forth to fill out our collections.

Skach ki was a game that we played in the middle of the street with two sticks of wood. The object of the game was to hit a small stick with a big one, usually a broomstick. There were many rules, and we played in teams against other boys in the summers.

In the winter we went sledding and threw snowballs. We had fun until I threw a snowball into a moving car and the driver turned around to chase me. I ran fast, but he was faster and caught me. I cried in fear and was lucky that he had pity on me and let me go. Another time, I threw a stone at some kids and broke a window. I ran away, but the homeowner had recognized me. He caught me and gave me a beating; then he was arrested for hitting a child. The case went to court, he apologized to me, and the case was closed.

Many times we would grab onto horse-drawn sleds to be pulled along the street. One day, I came home with my younger brother after one of these expeditions, and he told our father that I had been hanging onto the sleds. My father gave me a beating with a rubber belt from his sewing machine. After he finished, I told him that my brother had done the same thing. He got a double beating, one for hanging onto the sled, and one for tattling. Yes, we had a lot of fun.

Like kids today, we wanted to imitate the grownups and decided to smoke. Cigarettes were prohibitively expensive, so we smoked matches. Some of the older boys bought a box of matches and lined them up end to end. They lit the first one, which ignited the second, and so on; we were supposed to inhale the sulfur fumes. I tried it once, but never again! To me, it was like the conductor's chloroform—a little went a long way!

The Daugava River, immensely long, started in Russia and flowed through Latvia and emptied into the Gulf of Riga and then the Baltic Sea. Barges carried cargo back and forth to the port. Islands of various sizes dotted the center of the river and two bridges crossed from the city to the largest islands. Some of the islands were inhabited, while others were just for lovers looking for privacy. During the winter, when the river was frozen solid, farmers would come down the river on sleds, just as if it were a road. Sometimes ice floes would float by with animals stranded on them. The river was quite dangerous; in the winter people sometimes fell through the ice, and in summer there were drownings. We used to watch the tugboat fishing the bodies out and saw them taken to the morgue.

Our house was a half-block from the river, where I learned how to swim between the barges during the summer. One summer a band of us boys decided to swim to one of the islands, nicknamed "Lover's Paradise." We bundled up our clothing and swam with one hand over our heads, holding up the bundle to keep the clothes dry. When we got to the shore, we dressed again and explored the island, then reversed the procedure to get home. Our parents would have been furious if they had known about our adventure, so we had to keep dry to hide the evidence.

Every year on Rosh Hashanah, all the Jews went down to the river for *Tashlik*, the ceremonial throwing away of sins, and fights always broke out with the non-Jews. To me, the holiday felt like a day of mourning, until one time some Jewish boys decided to step into the matter, and they made peace for a while.

We went to shul every Friday night and Shabbat morning, as well as on all the holidays. The main shopping district was right around the corner, and trolley car no. 5 passed through it. There was a candy store, a household goods store, a brush store, a bakery, a kosher butcher, and a barbershop. We all got the same haircut: a baldy—it was clean and cheap. The bathhouse was two blocks away, and we went every Friday. Afterward we had a treat, ice cream in the summer and Rubanankus lemon soda in the winter.

When I was nine, I contracted scarlet fever and was taken to the hospital. This was the first time in my life that I was left by myself. I was in an isolation ward, and they sent a squad to disinfect the house. I stayed in the hospital for two weeks. Only my parents were permitted to come and see me through the window. I noticed that my father had grown a beard, and couldn't understand why he hadn't shaved. When I was released and came home, I found out that his younger brother, Meyer, only twenty-eight, had died, and my father was in the thirty-day mourning period when a man isn't permitted to shave.

In Riga, the winters are long and cold, the summers short and hot. Winter sets in around October and lasts until May, with short days and long nights, whereas in summer the nights were short and the days long, with the sun setting after 10 P.M. The river used to freeze solid, and ice-cutters would cut huge squares of ice to store in warehouses for summer use.

My friend Joske Strugatz was my neighbor. We all went to school together, walking to Latzpleshiela on Moskowariela or along the river, where Joske fell in one winter day when I was ten or eleven. We carried schoolbags stuffed with many heavy books so that we could do our homework, which included Hebrew, geography, Latvian history, and math.

The river had frozen overnight, and although we knew it was dangerous, Joske and I decided to test the ice to see if it was solid enough to cut for storage. Joske put his school bag into his left hand and pushed it down hard on the ice to see if it was thick and strong enough to hold his weight. It held the bag, but when Joske put his weight on the ice as well, it cracked, and he went down into the freezing water with his books.

I started to pull him up, but he almost took me down with him. I begged him to let go of the briefcase to lighten his weight, but he wouldn't drop his books. I don't know how I managed to pull him up; it was a miracle that I succeeded. He was soaking wet, and I rushed him to his home. We told his

mother that he had fallen in a puddle of water, but she was suspicious because he was so wet. I said that he had gotten up and
fallen in again and again. In this way I saved his life and also
saved him from a beating.

We led on the whole a peaceful existence, even living in har-
mony with the non-Jews, until the invasion of the Russian army.
Even so, I did not personally feel pressure from the Russians to
change my lifestyle. I had graduated from grammar school just
before the Russians came, and I continued to take high school
classes at night, which continued under Russian rule. During
the day, I worked as a shipping clerk in the office of a fur
export-import company.

It was close to the Jewish holidays, but people had stopped
going to the synagogue because the atheistic Russian government frowned upon religious observance. When it was time for
my Bar Mitzvah around Hanukkah, my parents did not
arrange a celebration, except for cake and liquor served in the
synagogue during Saturday morning services.

The Russian government lasted one year and five days—and
then the Germans invaded us.

3

THE NAZIS ARRIVE IN RIGA

ON JUNE 17, 1940, THE RUSSIAN ARMY overran Latvia and occupied Riga. I continued to work in the beautiful office, located in the middle of the city, across the street from a famous park. The office was the front of the Zoltinsky apartment, where they lived with two of their three daughters, aged twenty-one and nineteen. The third daughter was married and lived with her husband and child in Belgium. The Zoltinskys were quite wealthy; they had a maid as well as a summer home near the Baltic Sea. Mr. Zoltinsky traveled a great deal on business, making trips to Russia, the United States, England, Belgium, and other countries.

A year later, on June 14, 1941, in the middle of the night, the Russians arrested Mr. and Mrs. Zoltinsky because they were "bourgeois," raped the two daughters and closed up the office. My job in the fur business was over.

I found another job in a car factory. I took apart motors so that they could rebuilt. I remained at that job for a week, until the war started on June 22, 1941.

I'll never forget the noise created by the air raid and fire sirens and the sound of the planes that were bombing Riga. The sounds are still inside of me. In Riga everyone was confused. No one knew if they should run or stay home. People were getting killed; fires burned all over from the bombings. The city firemen would race to put out the fires and then be killed in the air raids. Every day bombing runs occurred and the ambulances were very busy. It was chaotic. As time went on, fewer and fewer people remained in the city, including the Russian soldiers. I walked to work as long as my job lasted, whereas my older brother, Mendel, took the trolley car. But after the first few days of the shelling, Riga lost its electricity and the cars stopped running. Mendel now walked to work. No more transportation, no more telephone, and the city died. Just as they killed the people, they killed the city.

I was thirteen-and-a-half, my older brother was seventeen-and-a-half; my younger brother was twelve-and-a-half, not yet Bar Mitzvah. The two little ones were ten and one-year-old. One day Mendel went to work and never returned, and we never saw him again. I found out years later that he had been conscripted into the Russian army.

During the day people walked everywhere, to work, to visit friends, to try to shop, a near impossibility with all the closed businesses and shortages. Meanwhile, people were thinking about leaving Riga. They would go to the railroad station, hoping that the trains would soon leave, but the bombing by the German air force made it impossible for the trains to move. Buses waited to take women with small children out of the city, but we did not know their destination. Some people ran to the busses, which were quickly filled.

My father begged my mother to go on the bus, but she refused. She insisted upon waiting for my older brother to come home and remained with me and my brothers.

We heard many different war reports on the radio until the radio stations stopped broadcasting. Then, on the blackest of days, July 1, 1941, the German army occupied Riga. I was not quite fourteen. On that same day, I saw many people killed by the German soldiers, shot down in the streets by machine guns and army tanks.

The next day the Germans, with the help of our Latvian neighbors, surrounded and arrested thoousands of Jewish men, put them in jail, and shot them all. I was afraid to go into the streets and be arrested. On July 4, the order came from Berlin to burn the synagogues with the people in them. I was lucky that they didn't catch me, but my friend Menachem Steinman was caught and ordered to pour gasoline all around the synagogue and burn the Holy Scrolls along with the congregation inside. Our sexton, Reb Manes, who used to put the Holy Scrolls on the lectern, wrapped himself in his prayer shawl and was burned along with the Torah Scrolls. After my friend Menachem had finished pouring the gasoline the Germans forced him to go into the burning synagogue, and there he died.

The Gogol Street Shul, Riga's largest synagogue, destroyed with 500 Jews trapped inside, July 4, 1941

The Latvian collaborators caught about two hundred Jews on the street and pushed them into the famous Gogol Street Shul, joining three hundred Lithuanian refugees had been housed inside. The Latvians boarded up the doors so the prisoners could not escape and set fire to that edifice.

Sixty-four synagogues were burned on that infamous day, July 4, 1941. The Soviet government had closed the shuls and the Germans burned them, torturing their congregations with a terrible death. The only shul that was spared was the Petau Shul; it was not burned because it was surrounded by tall buildings, and there was a church nearby. The Latvians were afraid that if the Petau Shul burned, the fire would spread to the other buildings. Instead, the Germans used the shul as a livery stable.

In 1988, when I arrived in Riga for the first time since the war, my cousin was my guide, and he pointed out what had happened since the war. None of the shuls had been rebuilt in the intervening fifty years. We decided to create a monument on the spot where the Gogol Shul had been burned. After the war, the bodies of the victims had not been removed from the spot. The Soviets simply filled in the burned-out shell and cemented over the ground, leaving the corpses interred in the cellar, and opened a public garden on that site. We arranged for the stones of the shul to be made into a wall where the entrance to the shul used to be, and we called it the Wall of Tears.

The Nazis began to prepare the worst neighborhood in Riga, Moscower Forstadt, to be used as the Jewish ghetto, encompassing an area of approximately six blocks by two blocks on the outskirts of Riga. The non-Jewish Latvians who lived there were forced to move out so that the Jews could be ordered to move into the buildings.

When my parents realized that all the Jews would be forced into a ghetto eventually, they decided to move in before the orders came through. In this way they were able to choose an apartment; those people who were driven into the ghetto after-

The author and his wife in front of the Wall of Tears Memorial, built on the site of the Gogol Street Synagogue, June 1993

ward by the Nazis had no choice of where to live. Although the ghetto had been formed from the worst neighborhood in Riga, my father found a spacious and well-kept apartment at 37 Ludzasiela. On September 11, 1941, we exchanged apartments with the Latvians who lived there; they kept our furniture, and we kept theirs—they, naturally, made out better on this deal! We moved with only the personal belongings we could carry.

We had enough room for our family, and my father even took in a German Jewish couple who had fled to Riga after the Nazis came into power. They lived with us for some time, but when the *Aktionen* began, they committed suicide together, slashing their wrists rather than wait to be taken away by the Nazi murderers.

The ghetto streets were surrounded by triple stands of barbed wire, with a gate at Daugavasiela, and no one was permitted in or out without direct orders from the Germans.

On November 27, 1941, the Germans ordered the people in a square block on the eastern side of the ghetto to leave their apartments by nightfall. We didn't realize what was happening, until all of a sudden, a distant cousin of my father ran in. "Moshe, help me! The Germans are chasing us out of our homes!" We already had eight people in our apartment, but now we took in four more, two adults and two children.

The next day, all able-bodied men over sixteen were ordered to assemble at the gate. We hoped that the men were being assembled to work; my mother was very worried, because men were taken away every day to be held as hostages. The Germans kept a group of men imprisoned in the Riga jail and in case of any partisan activity, the hostages were shot. Ten Jews were selected from the cells, taken out to the nearby forest or cemetery, and murdered. However, the Germans had ordered this particular section cleared because they planned to isolate the able-bodied men in that area, which came to be known as "the small ghetto."

I felt that I could work alongside my father, although I was only fourteen. I took a chance and decided to go with the men. We never saw our home or joined our family again.

Into an assembly area not bigger than a basketball court, the Nazis squeezed between 2,000 and 4,000 people. We were not sure where we were going. Our guard showed up late so my father, his friend, and I left to work for the police department, but that night we were marched through the gate and turned right, into the small ghetto. Most of our few possessions had been left in the large ghetto, and we were unable to claim them. We had nothing but the clothes we wore and the belongings in our pockets, if any.

The area was surrounded by triple strands of barbed wire and the street running through the ghetto was now no-man's land. It was forbidden to cross it or to walk in the street without a guard.

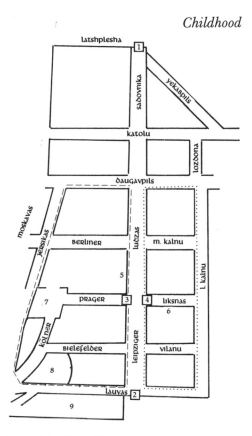

Map of the Riga Ghetto

The next night, November 29, 1941, we heard shooting and screaming. The small ghetto was surrounded with triple guards and barbed wire. They locked us into the house so we couldn't go to see what was happening. The screaming and shooting were unbearable and continued all night long. That night was a horror. For hours we heard shooting, shooting without end.

When we went to work the next morning, we found out that half of the ghetto population was gone. We didn't know where they were, but we had our suspicions. We had heard a rumor a few days earlier that Russian prisoners of war were digging graves in Rumbuli Forest, graves the size of two square blocks.

Yes, these were the graves of our dear ones, whom we never saw again.

Our families had been terrified that the men had been separated in order to be killed, but the reverse was true. Between November 30 and December 8, 1941, all the women, children, elderly, or sickly men were taken to Rumbuli Forest outside Riga or Biekernikke Forest and killed in grisly mass executions.

We looked through the barbed wire, afraid that our family had been killed, and our family was on the other side of the wire, afraid that the Germans had taken us to be killed. I spotted my brother on the other side of the fence, and he saw me at the same time. We talked to each other across no-man's land and planned to meet again the next day, but the guard chased him away from the fence. I thought that it might be possible to smuggle Leiser out of the big ghetto and keep him in the small ghetto with us, but I hesitated too long. Some people did manage to smuggle their young sons into the small ghetto before the main *Aktion*, but it was too late for Leiser.

We had hoped that the killings were over, but a few days later, on December 8, 1941, the Nazis chased the remaining women, children, and old men out of their homes and took them to be killed in Rumbuli Forest. The Latvian guards carried out the executions. As before, Russian prisoners had been forced to dig enormous trenches. Machine gunners were stationed at each corner of the graves, and the Nazis herded the victims to the edges of the open graves and shot them there. My mother and three younger brothers were among the victims.

We were shocked beyond measure and did not know what to do, since we were completely helpless. The instructions from Berlin stated that the killings were to stop at 1 P.M. on December 9. The German and Latvian murderers did their best to kill as many Jews as possible in that time period. Now that the large ghetto had been liquidated, the numerous doctors who had survived were not considered necessary to treat the remaining

Jews in the small ghetto. A bus destined for Rumbuli Forest was loaded with these doctors, and the Germans ordered it to drive away. The bus broke down, and the driver attempted to repair it, but he couldn't fix the damage, and the journey was again delayed.

The doctors knew that they were being taken to Rumbuli to be killed and decided to take poison rather than wait to be shot. As luck would have it, the order to stop the killings came through. Meanwhile, all of the doctors had taken the poison and half of them were already dead. The rest were taken back to the small ghetto to have their stomachs pumped. Ultimately, none of them survived.

But the Germans were not satisfied. The same day, they broke down the doors of every apartment in the ghetto to look for children. They shot everyone who got in their way. One boy ran away from the Nazis, fleeing over the roof, but they chased him. He tried to fly like a bird, leaping off the rooftop, and died in the courtyard. His body lay in the yard until his two uncles returned from work and took him away.

The next day the Germans selected twenty men from the small ghetto to collect the dead people in the two ghettos. Over 800 bodies of women, children, and aged men were dragged out on sleds to be burned and their remains thrown into a mass grave in the old cemetery adjoining the ghetto. Today the cemetery is a park, with no indication that Jewish victims of the Nazis are buried beneath the grass.

4

THE BIG GHETTO
AND THE SMALL GHETTO

WHEN WE WERE TAKEN into the big ghetto on December 9, we found the corpses of people who had been shot in the streets or in their homes and we removed the dead bodies. Some people in the hospital were still alive, but we couldn't smuggle them into the small ghetto because we were surrounded by guards and counted often. The following day the guards went back into the large ghetto and killed anyone they found alive.

My cousin Mottel's family was all killed. We learned the terrible truth from a woman who had been included in the purge at Rumbuli. She miraculously survived, struggled out from under the pile of corpses and crawled to a nearby farmhouse. The Latvian peasants hid her for two weeks, but were afraid to keep her longer for fear of retaliation by the Germans, so she donned men's clothing and joined a Jewish work crew which was returning to the ghetto under guard. Many inmates learned of the tragic deaths of their loved ones from her testimony.

By December 9, the big ghetto was empty, but not for long. On December 12, we saw people coming into the big ghetto. We wondered who they were and where they had come from, but for quite some time we couldn't find out. Finally, after several weeks, we heard that the elimination of the Jews of Riga had been part of the Nazi master plan. The ghetto had been cleared to make room for Jews from Germany, Austria, and Czechoslovakia, who were also slated for death. The Nazis had been impressed by the efficiency of the Latvians in eliminating their own Jews, and therefore these deportees had been sent to be killed by the Latvians as well. All this came out later in the testimony of a German officer at his war-crime trial.

The newcomers were settled in our homes, our apartments, without our knowledge or acquiescence. We were very depressed about what had happened to our families and our belongings. We felt that we had no future. The new arrivals didn't realize that they had been brought to the killing fields; they thought—or hoped—that they had been brought to Riga

Skirotavas Station, last stop for many German, Austrian, and Czech Jews

for resettlement. They didn't know that their sojourn in Riga would be very brief. Our emotions, already wounded by the killing of our dear ones, were freshly lacerated by seeing these new arrivals expecting to have a future in our ghetto.

Not all of the new arrivals were "resettled," even temporarily. The deportees were brought to Latvia by train, unloading at the Skirotavas Station on the outskirts of Riga. Most of them met the same fate as the murdered Riga Jews. They were taken immediately to the forests several kilometers from the station, forced to stand at the edges of the already-dug trenches, and killed by machine gun fire. In fact, six earlier transports were taken directly to various mass gravesites and shot. Some of the transportees walked, others were driven in busses. An eyewitness recalled seeing twenty-five bus loads of Jews per day being driven to Rumbuli and Biekernikke Forests for elimination.

The minority who remained were brought into the big ghetto, not far from the station, where the women and children were kept in the ghetto, and the men were taken daily to work with us. Some 20,000 non-Latvian Jews were killed between November 1941 and February 1942. Later transports were not brought into ghettos but immediately killed in the forests, where the bodies of the uncounted victims were buried.

The able-bodied German Jews took over some of the available jobs, especially those of camp police, carpenters, tailors, and shoemakers. Those who were fit for work received a meager food ration, but women and children, as well as men who didn't go out to work, didn't receive any food. The girls used to line the fence and stretch their hands into no-man's land as we returned from work to the small ghetto, piteously begging for something to eat. We shared our rations or the food we had traded for with the Latvians outside the ghetto, even though we never had enough even for ourselves.

We went through a terrible period both physically and mentally. In one week the Germans and their Latvian allies had

Tracks of Skirotavas Station, leading to the death pits in Rumbuli and Biekernikke Forests

killed approximately 30,000 Jews. On November 28, 1941, they had put us younger men into the small ghetto, separating us from the others after the first week, so that we could not organize a resistance and fight the German and Latvian guards. We were completely helpless and could do nothing but mourn for our lost families. Even our mourning was cut short. We were forced to return to work immediately, under penalty of instant death. Every night we came back to the ghetto lay down in bed and cried our eyes out.

Our apartment had three rooms, each with six beds. There was no electricity or running water in the house. The toilet was in the hall, and washing facilities consisted of a pump in the backyard. The yard held a stable, but no horses. The entrance to the apartment was in the fenced-in backyard, which was shared by another building with more apartments. We tried to keep clean to maintain our health, and washed ourselves in icy water, half-naked in the cold weather. Sometimes the water had frozen and we washed ourselves with snow. Such were our living quarters.

The few young men in the house, including myself, still tried to hold onto our youth. In order to keep up our spirits, we invented competitions among ourselves. One "event" was a test to see who could remain longest under the icy water of the pump.

Every man had a job in the city and whenever we went back to the ghetto we were required to walk in the street accompanied by a guard. He was quite friendly to us until we reached the ghetto gate, where we were searched for ammunition or other contraband. If the guards found anything "illegal," they would hang, shoot, or jail the unlucky victim.

I had performed manual labor in the barracks of the German soldiers, cleaning the toilets and sweeping the floor. No matter how hard the work, however, I found a fringe benefit. While sweeping, I would pick up the cigarette butts thrown down by the Germans, and my father would take them apart, remove the leftover tobacco, and make new cigarettes from them. In this way, he was able to smoke. Other men smoked anything available, even dried grass, since real cigarettes were impossible to obtain.

Not all of the soldiers were Germans; soldiers from Fascist Spain joined forces with the Nazis, and some were assigned to Riga. Those soldiers suffered terribly from the cold; coming from the warm Mediterranean region, they were unaccustomed to our arctic weather and found it very difficult to acclimatize. I would see them huddled over the stove, or miserably walking about the compound, huddled into their coats in a vain attempt to warm up.

My father and I had worked as tailors. With another man, we made uniforms for the police department. We had enough food, and whenever they finished a garment, the policemen celebrated with vodka to try to make my father drunk. I was afraid to let my father drink too much and get into trouble, so I used to drink part of his portion of the vodka. In this way the police department forced a fifteen-year-old boy to become a drunk.

After a short time, the other man decided he wanted a girl-friend of his from the large ghetto to work as a police tailor. The work was allotted to three people only, so he forced me out to make room for his girlfriend. My father remained there until the summer, when he was sent to work in the swamps, but I was assigned other work.

The Nazis had eliminated my father's tailoring job for the summer, so he was taken to work in the bogs around Riga, digging up turf which was dried for fuel. The conditions were very bad; the barracks were surrounded by barbed wire, and the air was unhealthy. He worked from morning till night for two months; then he came back to the small ghetto, until one day he was sent to a work camp called Lenta.

While my father worked in the turf-cutting commando, he witnessed an act of unspeakable cruelty by the notorious Eduard Roschmann, the Butcher of Riga. One morning, two of the young men who were assigned to cut turf came late to *Appell* (roll call). For this infraction, Roschmann shot them dead as they stood in line.

My father was devastated by this cruel act. One of the young men was Arthur Kaufman, the son of his good friend, Max, and my father was very close to him. In addition, he couldn't help but think, "This could have been my own son". He lived in fear that something would happen to me, his only surviving child, whereas on my part, I worried constantly about his condition in the bogs. We were both helpless. All we could do was hope for a miracle that would allow us to be reunited.

I had to go to an open-air market in the now-empty main ghetto and line up with other unemployed Jews, while foremen chose workers from the selection in the marketplace.

The work assignments varied. Sometimes I carried water pipes or unloaded trains at the railway station. I did not look like a teenager and worked just as hard as any of the grown men. When we worked on the railroad, we had a crew of twenty men, Latvian Jews, and two women, German Jews.

The women worked in the office with the German soldiers, but they usually returned to the camp with us. Sometimes they didn't come with us, but instead stayed overnight with the German soldiers. They were beautiful girls, but as hungry as the rest of us; by sleeping with the soldiers they procured enough food for themselves and their families.

Because our job of unloading pipes took us all over the city, we were sometimes permitted to ride back on the trains—in boxcars, of course. When we rode with the girls, they spoke kindly to me because I was the youngest of all the men. When the ride home was very long, they whiled away the time by teaching me how to dance.

Finally, I was assigned as part of a group to do manual labor at Goeginger, a factory that manufactured and packaged delicacies such as chocolates and herring, which were intended for the German troops. As well as other manual tasks, my job entailed loading trucks with barrels of the delicacies.

My father returned to the small ghetto for a short period before he was sent to the labor camp named Lenta. I worked in the factory until the small ghetto was eliminated, and then I was sent to Lenta, too, where I rejoined my father.

The Silent Witness
and His Master

The Silent Witness, my silver ring

I was born in the year 1942,
Together with a first cousin and some friends.
My father was a silver spoon
Whereas my cousin's father was a silver teaspoon
And my friends' fathers were a silver spice box
And a silver Kiddush cup.
All this happened in the ghetto in Riga, Latvia.
My master lost his mother and three of his brothers on
    December 8, 1941,
Yet we remained inseparable
The entire time until the war ended.
Together we were in various concentration camps.
In October 1944 my master was sent to Stutthof,
An infamous concentration camp,

Where he was stripped of all his belongings,
Meager though they were,
Yet he managed to hang on to me
Throughout the eight weeks he suffered there.
I was nearly sold for a loaf of bread
But was rescued by my master's father,
Who traded gold for this bread.
A second time I was rescued by his father
When he removed his gold teeth with pliers
To trade again for bread.
My master's cousin and friends sold my look-alikes
Who were also silent witnesses.
I was lucky to remain with my master
Until we were liberated by the Russian army, March 10,
    1945.
My master was stricken with typhus
Yet he kept me with him throughout this time
Although he did not know if he would live.
I came to the United States with my master;
He is married and had offspring.
I became a partner to his three children,
And he took me to Israel many times.
I lived to see Israel born and flourish.
During my time I have seen Jews
Killed, tortured, shot, sick, hungry, burned,
And also happy.
I was invited to be a display
In the archives of a museum of the Holocaust,
Both in Israel and in the United States.
My master, however, refused to be separated from me.

The Four Rings

My four rings

I have four rings: the silver ring that I had made in Riga ghetto in August 1942; my wedding ring that I was married with on June 4, 1950; my father's wedding ring, from his second marriage on December 31, 1945; and the ring I was given on my fiftieth birthday, December 26, 1977.

The ring I had made in the ghetto has its own tale, woven into the true story of the Riga ghetto.

My wedding ring gave me a fruitful life and a beautiful *Aishes Chayil* for a wife, plus three nice educated children and smart grandchildren.

My father's wedding ring reminds me of his marriage; there was no one left from the family to give him a blessing. My father and his wife started their married life in Germany and later came to the United States. Finally, they went to live in Israel. My father died December 8, 1982, exactly forty-one years to the day from the date when my mother and brothers were killed in Rumbuli Forest. He said Kaddish for his sons and my mother for all that time.

After he passed away, my stepmother gave me his ring; I wear it every day with the other two rings. The silver ring has its place of honor in my home.

My silver ring is my lucky charm, which keeps all my rings together as a family, because I no longer have brothers, and my wife lost her sister. But the ring keeps our future together with our children and grandchildren. We have pleasure, health, and *nachas*.

5

LENTA

DURING OUR DAYS IN THE SMALL GHETTO, we wanted to live like normal teenagers. Family life had been disrupted; the small ghetto held only men, and the large ghetto mainly women. The young male deportees mostly had been taken to Salaspils, the nearby death camp, where they were used in experiments. Gradually, some of the men in the small ghetto found ways to visit the women across no-man's land. The men were interested in sex, and the women complied in order to obtain food. I was too young to be interested in sex, and I still wanted to feel like a kid. I had an idea that I would like to have a ring.

Naturally, under normal circumstances, anyone who wants a ring just goes into a jewelry shop and selects one from the showcase. Our situation was somewhat different. We teens had formed a group, and in October 1942, we decided to have rings made. We hoped to survive and wanted to have a keepsake from home. Mr. Lurie, the silversmith, told us to bring him any type of silver item—a spoon, a Kiddush cup, a spice box, a knife, or anything else, and he would melt the silver and make rings to our measurements. He said he could put our Hebrew initials on the face of the ring, and the date our families were killed on the inside, as a memorial.

I took our last silver teaspoon to Mr. Lurie, and he made the spoon into a ring. Other boys had rings made from other silver objects. We were so proud of our rings, symbolic of membership in our group. I still have my ring, and someday it will rest in the United States Holocaust Museum in Washington, D.C.

Whenever I talk to schoolchildren, I tell them about my ring, and I point out that people wear rings that have personal significance to them, like class rings, team rings, engagement and wedding rings, etc. My ring represents my life during the war; most of the rings that were made in the ghetto are gone, along with their owners. The fact that my ring and I survived together is nothing short of miraculous.

On October 25, 1942, the Germans discovered that some prisoners had formed a resistance movement and had smuggled ammunition into the small ghetto from the Pulverturm, the German ammo dump.

They broke into our apartment in the middle of the night, drove us out, and assembled us in the ghetto. The Gestapo formed five groups, and we were interrogated by each group through the night. We were taken through the ghetto's three checkpoints and at each one, we had to "prove" that we were physically fit: We had to remove our caps, replace them, perform calisthenics, and run an obstacle course. At each interrogation point they separated the "unfit" Jews from the main group and loaded them into trucks.

Ultimately, 150 men were selected as unfit and executed. We lost two men from our apartment, Mr. Blum and Mr. Herzberg. It was a terrible shock to us all, but we had no alternative but to think about the future, and in the morning we obeyed when we were ordered to go to work. When we returned from work that day we heard shots and later found out that the Nazis had killed all forty-one of the Jewish policemen as well.

Pulverturm: German storage site from which ammunition was stolen by the resistance, leading to the death of the 41 Jewish policemen and 150 others

The Nazis decided that both the big and small ghettos would be eliminated in the near future. I knew the head of the small ghetto, because I had worked with his brother-in-law in the factory, and he promised to send me to Lenta, the work camp where my father had been sent earlier. He kept his word and sent me to join my father in May 1943, and we were together until the liberation. Both of the ghettos were closed on November 2, 1943. The sick or "unfit" who remained in the ghettos were sent directly to the gas chambers and crematoria at Auschwitz or Kaiserwald.

What to do with European Jewry? When Hitler came to power in Germany he attempted to destroy the German Jews by taking away their businesses and property and putting them into concentration camps. When the war started, the German army occupied the Baltic countries, Lithuania, Latvia and Estonia. They arrested the Jews and began killing them. Within one year Latvia was virtually *judenrein* ("Jew-clean"). The "useful" Jews, mostly men, were forced to work or were taken for experiments. The Nazis performed many kinds of cruel and inhuman experiments on the Jews, mainly as endurance tests, both physical and mental.

For example, they forced men to wear shirts filled with lice for weeks at a stretch. They wanted to see the reaction of people who were tortured by the lice, and to see the effects of temperature changes on the vermin. The victims were human guinea pigs; the experiment was supposedly performed to evaluate how the soldiers on the front lines would react in the same situation and to find ways to combat louse infestations.

In another experiment, they sprayed young men with cold water for some time, forced them to have sex with women, and then sprayed them with cold water again. This would go on until the men collapsed.

Another experiment involved the weather. They wanted to test human beings for endurance in the cold, supposedly so that when the German army faced the Russians in the winter, they would know how much to expect from their soldiers. They kept Jews outside in extremely cold weather, as well as in very hot conditions, to see how long they could function. They were tested and retested until they collapsed and died. Sometimes the Nazis would force people to perform the same mental task all day long, to see if they would break down from the pressure.

They also forced the Jews to help them remove the evidence of their atrocities. Young men were selected to disinter the corpses of people who had been shot and buried in mass graves. The arms and legs of the young men were chained together so that they could not escape from the area where the digging took place. While they worked, the manacles were removed from their arms so they could swing their shovels and only their feet were shackled. They had to line up the bodies, place a row of timber over them, and repeat till all the bodies were covered with wood. Then they set fire to the pyre so that the grave would be cleared.

This was why the Nazis did not kill all the Jews outright. They wanted to perform their inhuman experiments on us, and they wanted us to do their dirty work. They claimed their disgusting experiments were to further the quest for knowledge for the future good of mankind, but in reality they were simply indulging their sadistic pleasures.

By the end of the war they were moving us around to different places, different cities, different countries. Eventually we wound up doing nothing for days and weeks, while people died of hunger, sickness, exhaustion, or murder. The Germans almost accomplished what they had set out to do: wipe out all the Jews of Europe. As it was, they murdered six million Jews and countless other people.

During my seventeen months in Lenta, we were always under threat of death by firing squad. People never knew what would happen to them and were almost powerless. Nevertheless, a few of us miraculously survived.

I arrived in the work camp in May 1943, before the Riga ghetto was liquidated. Fritz Scherwitz (Elke Sirewitz) was in charge as Obersturmführer. It was tough to be a young teenager without a trade in Lenta since almost everyone sent there had a profession of some kind. I wanted to go to Lenta because my father worked there. We had been separated when he was taken to Lenta to perform his work as a tailor.

Five hundred Jewish men and women worked in Lenta, tradesmen, tailors, shoemakers, carpenters, mechanics, butchers, doctors, musicians, and so on. The musicians were ordered to perform concerts at night to entertain the ss.

Within two months of my arrival one hundred Jews had been taken away to be shot, reducing the population by twenty percent. The Germans claimed that there was not enough work for unskilled laborers, and the victims were not doing "important" jobs. They were loaded onto trucks, driven into the forest, and shot. Among those taken was a friend with whom I had arrived in Lenta.

The remaining men slept in a tremendous hall equipped with double bunk beds. Each of us had a box next to his bunk, which we called a night table. Each prisoner kept his personal belongings in the box, such as can of sugar or salt, a spoon, a razor with a shaving brush and personal articles. People stored extra food there when they could get it. Coffee was served at breakfast time, lunch consisted of soup, and supper was bread with margarine, salt and sugar. We showered once a week in a shack near the kitchen We ate and slept in the same hall, and the evening concerts were also given there.

The after-dinner concerts were conducted for the relaxation of the ss officers. Cantor Shelkon was our singer, accompanied by Abraham Shapiro on the violin. Another man played Bach on the piano, and a cellist completed the "orchestra."

When I first came to Lenta I worked as a manual laborer, cleaning the streets, washing toilets, and taking out garbage. After a while I was assigned to work in the kitchen, where I made a good impression on the head cook.

I worked seven days a week, rising at 3 A.M. to prepare hot water for tea and coffee for the 6 A.M. breakfast. One morning I sleepily stumbled against the huge kettle and burned my arm. To this day I still carry the scar on my forearm. After breakfast I cleaned the utensils and helped prepare for lunch, and after lunch helped prepare the supper. During the day I managed to catch a few hours of sleep. I worked in the kitchen until Lenta was liquidated in September 1944, and witnessed many tragic incidents.

Lenta Work Camp

I was very lucky because the director of the kitchen staff said he needed me, and thus again I miraculously avoided the firing squad.

After two months, four hundred Jews were left in Lenta, all Latvians. After a few months, a new transport arrived, but the newcomers were not Latvian. They were German, Czechoslovakian, Austrian, and Polish Jews. Some of the foreign Jews were from the Riga ghetto; the Polish Jews had come straight from Poland. Lenta now had a mixed Jewish population. Hitler's orders resulted in the intermingling of Jews from all over Europe. We were brought together and kneaded like dough into a suffering mass. At every turn, the mass became smaller and smaller, until in the end, only a few were still alive.

Included in the transport from the large ghetto was a family consisting of two brothers, a father, and another man named

Moshe Danziger. Many years later, I was reunited with the brothers, after the World Gathering of Holocaust Survivors. My friend Leo Kram also referred me to a man who had written saying that he had been in Lenta. I remembered him, but we had become separated after the liberation, when he moved to South America and later settled in Paris. His brother is a scientist who lives in Israel, and my wife and I had the honor to lunch with him.

Moshe Danziger looked like a skeleton when he first came to Lenta; I fed him extra food from the kitchen until he regained his health. After the war I met him again as I was passing through Germany, but afterward we lost touch. Years later, as a TV repairman, I made a service call to someone named Danziger. Sure enough, it was Moshe! We hugged and kissed, delighted to have met again. He recently died of cancer. I met his daughter in Jerusalem and told her that I had known her father for many years. She insisted that I tell the story to her already-grown children, so that they should learn what their grandfather had gone through.

All the police personnel in the camp were German Jews, including the head of the police department, a Herr Levy from Munich. A house located near the kitchen had been converted for use as a hospital. The doctor in the hospital was a German Jew, and his wife served as his nurse. Although the doctor collaborated with the Nazis to some extent, he did what he could to help his fellow Jews. The hospital had both inpatients and outpatients, as well as some chronic cases. One of my friends had leukemia; there was no medication to help him, so he didn't last too long.

I knew that my survival might depend on others, so I took every chance to make friends in important places. I managed to supply the doctor and his wife with leftover food. I even supplemented the rations of the police department and the patients in the hospital. I made sure that no food was thrown away. The only people I couldn't help were the German Jews who were painters, carpenters, and the like. They worked at their trades all day, so I had no way to get food to them, and all they had to eat was the meager food ration.

Since the Latvian Jews spoke Latvian, German, and Russian, we were in touch with the general Latvian population, and sometimes were fortunate enough to communicate with friends and neighbors. The German and Czech Jews were completely cut off from the rest of the world. We managed to do some trading with the Latvians, exchanging gold, diamonds, Russian coins, anything we could, for food. Anyone who was caught doing this, God forbid, was immediately taken away and shot. During Fritz Scherwitz's time, it was not so bad; the ss were in charge, so everything was done "by the book." When other ss officers were put in charge, especially the dog handlers, many people were caught and killed.

Life in Lenta was better than in other camps, however, for two reasons. First, Fritz Scherwitz was less inhumane than other commandants were. Second, most of the prisoners had skills that the Germans could exploit, so they kept us alive. We all had a place to sleep and food to eat, but if anyone were to get out of line, he was finished.

As Latvians who had lived in Riga, we spoke Latvian, and had connections with the outside. Every day, trucks left the camp with completed uniforms and other material, and the Jews involved in the deliveries arranged to trade hidden valuables with the Latvians outside the camp. I was sometimes in a position to find or trade for valuables in camp, and as a tailor, my father had a connection with the drivers and deliverymen on the outside. Between us we had organized an ongoing business.

On one occasion, two Latvian Jews made the delivery, took a prearranged detour to trade their valuables with a non-Jew for food, and then returned to Lenta. A German Jew who was with them was jealous of the arrangement because he could not trade with the Latvians. He reported the others to Scherwitz, who took immediate action.

The three young Jews were ordered to start digging their own graves behind the main building near the fence. Scherwitz then took the two Latvian Jews aside and advised them to kill the German Jew because he was an informer. Within minutes they took their shovels and started digging, but almost immediately they began chasing the German Jew with their shovels. Soon he was bleeding from the head; he was chased like a mouse to be killed. When he fell to the ground the men attacked him, and a few minutes later he was dead. He was put into a crate, and the official record showed that he had fallen off the roof. Then Scherwitz canceled the order to kill the two Latvian Jews.

Yes, this was the way Fritz Scherwitz conducted himself. He saved the rest of the Jewish population of Lenta from being shot or possibly transported to the concentration camp Kaiserwald. He didn't like squealers and took action against them. We were in Lenta until two weeks before the Russians took over Riga, and we felt lucky that Fritz Scherwitz was our commandant, because during his tenure he saved Jews. We later found out that Scherwitz was himself a Polish Jew.

When Fritz Scherwitz left on vacation, they brought in a genuine Nazi, the infamous Eduard Roschmann, to run Lenta. He was cruel and evil and always walked through the camp with his dog, an English boxer. As soon as he came into power, we found that people were missing, and we never knew what had happened to them. They never came back. One who disappeared overnight was the man who had been my teacher in the private school in Riga. The sense of danger under this regime made me feel as if I were facing a firing squad all the time.

Since I worked in the kitchen in Lenta, I became a "chemist." I took horse fat, beef fat and bacon, melted them together with onions, and created a spread to smear on bread. One day Roschmann came into the barracks with his dog. The dog smelled something unusual and pulled his master over to my locker where I had hidden my food. The ss officer forced me to empty all the food from my locker and called the doctor in from the next building to taste the food to find out why it had such an unusual smell.

The doctor, who was my friend because I had often supplied him extra food, gave me a wink as he tasted the food and reported that the odor came from onions. But the Nazi wanted to know how it came about that I had so much food and fats in my locker, since the food allowance was only enough for one or two days, at most. I told him that the food was not only my own, but I was also holding rations for my father and his friend.

He then ordered the chief of police, a German Jew, to bring my father to the kitchen. My father was forced to run down a few flights of stairs so that the Nazi should not have long to wait. When asked what he did with his ration of food, my father unhesitatingly replied, "Me? All my food goes to my son." The Nazi walked out, and that time I emerged the winner with my life. Once again I was rescued from the firing squad, this time by my father's quick thinking.

The doctor was always on our side, he helped us if he could. If the Nazis found out that a woman was pregnant, they killed her immediately, so the doctor performed life-saving abortions. There were no facilities for this operation, but the doctor used the primitive "hospital" that was set up in a few rooms in the house near the kitchen.

A few months later, the commandant invited other Nazis to come to Lenta to learn how to torture Jews. The ss suspected that ammunition had been smuggled into the camp by the resistance, and they decided to search everything. Whoever was suspected would be taken out of camp and shot. In the middle of the night we were roused from our beds and lined up outside.

They selected a few young men to work, and segregated the barbers and painters from the rest of the prisoners.

The barbers were ordered to shave the heads of all the prisoners, including the women, and the painters were instructed to paint large X's over everyone's clothing. This was to make it more difficult for us to escape.

The Nazis proceeded methodically and systematically, as usual. The young men were ordered to rip apart everything in the barracks, including the beds and lockers. Everything they found was separated and relocated. Salt, sugar, and other foods were sent to the kitchen, and everything else stored in the warehouse.

As a kitchen worker, I received the salt and sugar containers and was supposed to empty them into larger tubs. As I emptied the containers, I realized that one of them still felt heavy. I pried open the cover with my pliers and lifted it out. Inside I discovered that the can had a false bottom, which held a golden watch, a gold cigarette case, and rings. I discussed it with my father, and we realized that because we could not know which merchandise belonged to which prisoner, everything now belonged to me. Later my father was able to sell the gold items for meat and whiskey. The Germans had taken everything away from the Jews, and here again we had gold! It was a miracle which helped us to survive. One German had an expression, "You can undress a Jew naked and throw him into a river, and he'll come out on the other side completely dressed!"

The Gestapo did not find any ammunition, and once again I was saved from the firing squad.

We lived in this way until July 28, 1944, when we were ordered on a death march to Salaspils, a torture camp. Scherwitz attempted to save some of "his" Jews from the order that had come from Berlin. He had been ordered to send all the Jews to Germany because all the camps were to be liquidated.

He felt that we had a chance to survive at Salaspils, although it was a notorious death camp.

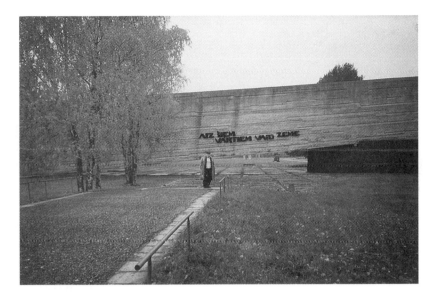

Salaspils Death Camp.
The inscription reads, "The earth moans beyond this gate"

As a kitchen worker, I was able to save up some bread. To keep the bread from spoiling, I again became a "chemist." I dried bread in the oven, and it became hardtack, which I packed into a bag. We were not told our destination, merely ordered to leave the camp. We assembled in the camp courtyard and marched out. We marched through the city of Riga and continued our death march until we reached Salaspils. We were not sure we would survive the march; many people died on the way, and those of us who remained were sure that we would be killed.

6

SALASPILS AND LENTA AGAIN

SALASPILS WAS A DEATH CAMP in the middle of the forest where more than 100,000 people, including 7,000 children, lost their lives. Salaspils existed under a reign of terror from October 1941 until September 1944. Most of the inmates were political prisoners or prisoners of war, although the Germans had experimented there with German Jewish men, who seldom returned to the ghetto from Salaspils.

We were shocked by the horrible sight that greeted us when we arrived in Salaspils in the afternoon: Thousands upon thousands of Russian prisoners of war were standing in a field. They were not working. They were not resting or eating. They were simply starving to death.

Some prisoners were assigned the job of moving a sand mountain. The procedure they followed was simple: every worker had a shovel, and they surrounded the mountain. Two prisoners held a flat wooden board between them like a stretcher and those with shovels loaded the flats with sand. After the stretcher was loaded, the bearers carried it around the mountain, making a trail the shape of a figure eight, and dumped out the sand. Lines and lines of people stretched into the distance like a coiled snake. That was how they moved a mountain at Salaspils.

This went on all day until midnight and began again early in the morning. People fell down from weakness, not having been fed, and other prisoners loaded them onto wagons. They disappeared, and we never, ever saw them again.

We spent eight terrible days in Salaspils. We slept in tents in the courtyard and lived outside like animals, we slept in tents, we were filthy, crawling with lice, and we did not wash for the entire three weeks. The Russian prisoners who stood outside in the field dropped like flies. My father and I were fortunate that the ss did not know we were related, because one or both of us would have been killed. Again, by a miracle I was saved from the firing squad.

We were ordered to return to Lenta, and of course, were carefully counted before the march and at its end. Three Jewish youths had escaped along the way, but they were soon captured and shot. Scherwitz lost his power to help the Jews from Lenta. Eighty were taken to the port city Libau. A hundred and five prisoners were taken away to concentration camp Kaiserwald for a "special" assignment. They were formed into the Kartoffelkommando ("potato unit"), whose job was to disinter the corpses of the victims buried in mass graves and burn the bodies. The Germans wanted to destroy the evidence of their barbarism because the Red Army was getting close, and they didn't want these masss graves discovered. Of course, the members of the Kartoffelkommando did not survive their gruesome assignment. Once again, by a miracle, my father and I were spared.

This was a horrible period, but then the Germans decided to move us again. On September 26, 1944, just two weeks before the Russians captured Riga, we were shipped to an unknown destination. We had no choice but to follow the instructions we were given, packed our belongings and were again ready to leave. We were ordered into trucks and driven by night to the port of the city of Riga.

We were forced out of the trucks and instructed to load a ship that was docked nearby. We became longshoremen, loading the ship all night and all the next day and through the next night until the dock was cleared, and the ship was loaded. We did not know the reason for the hurry, but later heard that the Russian front was quickly approaching Riga. Although we were ordered to board the ship, we did not sail for several hours. As the vessel moved away from the pier, we heard shots behind us, but we did not react. Gunfire meant nothing to us by then, because it seemed that every few minutes someone was shot.

Years later, I found out that there had been a fight between Roschmann and a German army officer, and Roschmann shot the other. The ship that we had loaded was the last one out of Riga by the Baltic Sea, and everyone was trying to escape, including even the German officers. This episode is used as a central incident in Frederick Forsythe's best-seller, *The Odessa File*.

The ship was loaded with people and matériel. Prisoners were brought in by the thousands from various concentration camps. To my amazement, I was reunited with my cousin Mottel, whom I hadn't seen after I was sent to Lenta.

Men and women together were driven down to the lowest level of the ship; we slept on metal grates, ate and maintained toilet facilities in the same place. The stench was unbearable; people were sick from the smell. In their weakened condition, people died, and their bodies were thrown overboard. To make matters worse, we were all seasick after we reached the open sea and to top it off, we were subjected to bombings from the Russian air force.

It was Yom Kippur the night the boats left Riga, and my friend Cantor Shelkon and I davened *Kol Nidre* down in the ship's hold. The atmosphere was very tense as we prayed to be

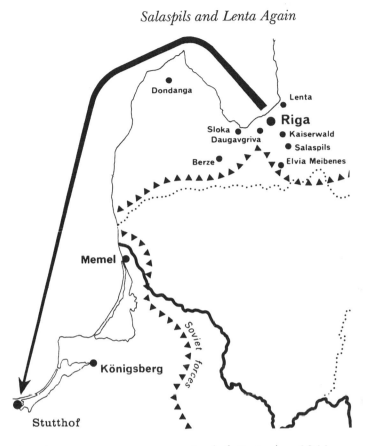

Map showing evacuation route to Stutthof, September, 1944

written down "for life and not for death" in the coming year. We prayed without *Machzorim* (holiday prayer books), reciting the five Yom Kippur services from memory throughout the terrible day. Once again, we pulled through by a miracle.

I was lucky because I had saved enough hardtack from the Lenta kitchen to last us for the three-day journey. I shared my bread with the other prisoners until we reached the port city of Danzig (now Gdansk, Poland). We were ordered to unload the ship, which took a day and a night, and again we did not know what would come next.

We picked up our belongings as ordered and marched to the Vistula River not far from the port. There we saw several empty barges waiting on shore, and the guards ordered us to climb aboard. They whipped us and pushed us until we were squeezed into the barges like sardines in a can, men and women together. We stood in the same spot on those barges for a day and a night, in the autumn sun and in the cold night rain. Finally we arrived at the infamous Stutthof concentration camp. Gestapo guards awaited us and ordered us to disembark as quickly as possible. A low voice ordered, *"Ausladen* [Get out]" and we had to get out of the barges. Some people fell into the water while some managed to get onto dry land.

Finally we formed a line to walk to κz Stutthof. We passed a line of English and American prisoners walking the other way. They had tears in their eyes as they looked at us, knowing that very few would come out of the hellhole we were entering.

INTERLUDE

Stutthof, the Horror Camp

I SPOKE AT THE Flatbush Park Jewish Center during the Yom HaShoah Memorial in 1993, and read a poem that was written in Yiddish. The audience had a large proportion of survivors and their families, and I said, "This poem is not only about me, it's also about you. Ladies and gentlemen, I had you in mind. It's your poem except for one word: the name of the concentration camp. My camp was Stutthof. Yours may have been Auschwitz, Dachau, Majdanek, Mauthausen, Treblinka, Bergen-Belsen, Buchenwald, Kaiserwald or any one of many many more. Wherever survivors gather, you can see people from all these camps. But when the name Stutthof is mentioned, there is seldom a response. That's because very few people ever left Stutthof alive. My father and I were among the few who miraculously survived Stutthof

"I wrote this poem in Yiddish, because we are Jews, and this was the language we spoke in the camps until Hitler and his hangmen killed us out except for the few of us who survived. Yiddish should not be forgotten and should live forever."

The poem has been translated in English to reach a broader audience. KZ stands for Konzentrationslager (concentration camp). The sentiments it expresses are common to all Holocaust survivors, whatever camps they suffered through, and people must learn of our experiences.

> I am a KZ survivor from Riga, Latvia. These are my memories of the suffering that I endured in KZ Stutthof in Germany.
>
> Arriving in Stutthof we could hardly think.
> We were in the dark and overnight we aged.
>
> They took away all our possessions, even the pictures of
>   our family,
> From that time on, a good day never came.
>
> They stripped off our clothes; they took away our garments,
> Replaced by prisoner's garb that we wore night and day till
>   our liberation.
>
> We wore wooden shoes and we couldn't walk quickly.
> They clattered on the ground like grim music.
>
> In the barracks where we slept were only beds,
> And many terrible things happened at night.
>
> On the bottommost tier of the bed four people slept,
> And everyone had lice without number.
>
> In the middle and top, people slept three by three,
> And each bed had another close by.
>
> The enemy, the Nazis and kapos, tortured us every night
> And choked out that we would not see the next morning.
>
> Every morning we were counted row after row.
> They wanted to make sure that each of us would participate.

In winter we stood for hours in the street—
This was not for our pleasure.

We stayed in the Appelplatz and could go nowhere.
We had to watch how Jews were hanged there.

We stayed in line all day to get a little to eat,
Now and forever we will never forget.

The coffee in the morning was watery
And just like our lives there, it was very bitter.

The soup was full of sand and water,
And we ate that in the street, all soaking wet in the rain.

Every day and night I thought,
"This not the life that God intended for me."

People committed suicide on the electric wire fence—
The end of life came fast on the spot without another step.

Eight weeks we were here, living through dark days and
    nights,
And they treated us worse than slaves.

The day we finally came out of Hell
Was the day our hopes were reborn.

How can I forget, and how can you forget, it's impossible. We
can't forget and we can't forgive the Nazis, the Germans, for
what they did to us Jews.

7

STUTTHOF

WHAT IS STUTTHOF? Stutthof is a notorious concentration camp in Germany, and now memorialized in Washington, D.C., and in Israel. In Germany Stutthof is two days travel by tugboat and barge from the port city of Gdansk. In Washington, Stutthof is part of the U.S. Holocaust Museum exhibit. And in Israel, Stutthof is inscribed at Yad Vashem as one comes to the display with all the infamous, notorious concentration camps, where the memorial flame burns night and day forever.

Unfortunately, very few survivors of Stutthof exist. It was known for torture, murder, and suicide. I was very lucky to survive with my father, living through eight weeks there. The day we arrived, we passed through the huge gate with the motto *"Arbeit Macht Das Leben Frei"* inscribed over it. We had marched in with our meager belongings after our journey from Riga, first by boat through the Baltic Sea, zigzagging through the minefields and under bombardment by the Russian air force, until we reached Danzig, and then by barge and on foot, till we walked through the dreaded gate at KZ Stutthof.

Very few people still had relatives—brothers, sisters, parents, or spouses—and we did not tell our captors that we were father and son for fear one or both of us would be killed. My father gave the name "Racs" while I used the spelling "Ratz" and we were fortunate that the Germans did not make the connection. The moment we came through the gates, men and women were separated, husbands and wives were torn apart, and many never saw each other again.

They ordered us to line up and strip off our clothing. We were not yet aware that this would be the last time we would wear those clothes, and that all our belongings, including our few family photographs, would be taken away from us forever. We all followed the order to undress; we were each allowed to keep a shaving brush, a razor, and a spoon. Luck was with me, and I was able to keep my silver ring, which I had worn since our time in the Riga ghetto. Everyone tried to keep something, to smuggle through one or two items that they felt were most important. My father smuggled through his hernia support belt, in which he had hidden some gold and diamonds.

Almost naked, we began to walk toward a large building with a sign designating it a Bathhouse. We had heard of the bathhouses that were really death showers, but we had no choice in the matter. We were lucky that this time there was water instead of gas; we were also provided with some ersatz soap. We were only allowed a few minutes in the shower; then they chased us to another building because the next group was waiting to wash.

We were given prisoners' clothing, including beret, undershirt, underpants, jacket, pants, coat, and shoes with wooden soles and canvas uppers. The jacket, pants, and coat were striped blue and white. We had no socks; we used paper instead, which came in handy for two reasons: It took up room in the shoes so that they fit better, and it also helped keep us warm. The clothing had been issued without regard to the size of the prisoner, and we looked and felt ludicrous; some of us wore clothing far too big, and others had clothes much too small. After we left the clothing barrack, we started exchanging garments with each other. I wore those same garments for five months, day and night, until liberation by the Russian army.

After an hour or so, we finally finished with the showers and garment issue and exchange. Barbers were sent in to shave all our heads so that we were completely bald. We learned that this was to minimize louse infestation: the less hair, the fewer lice. We were each issued a bowl, but we received nothing to eat. Now we each had a bowl, spoon, razor, and shaving brush.

My father had made a fabric pouch for me, which I wore around my neck on a string. I had my few possessions in the pouch, and even carried my father's spoon in it, but not our bowls. I carried the bowls tied around my waist with a piece of twine.

Another barrack waited for us: our sleeping quarters. The barrack had a public latrine with five commodes and five urinals to accommodate three hundred men. There were thirty rows of triple-tiered beds, 30 inches wide, each holding ten people. Four slept on the bottom tier, three in the middle, and three on top. We slept in this way for eight weeks, on straw mattresses, head to foot, smelling other people's feet and filthy clothes, and even sharing our lice. It was never quiet in the barrack; some people walked around all night long or slept in the bathroom to avoid the crowded bunks. Some people used the nights to try to steal from each other, so it was not safe to sleep; one had to safeguard his possessions. Whoever didn't watch his things could say goodbye to them. By order of the kapo, no one was permitted to walk outside until 4:30 A.M.

In Stutthof, the Jewish prisoners were on the bottom of the totem pole. The kapos, career criminals, were in charge. Each morning, the kapo would roust us from the barrack for a quick wash and a turn at the latrines, three hundred men vying for an opportunity in a facility meant for fifty. Then back in line for a bowl of ersatz coffee, endless roll calls, and a wait for further orders.

The first morning after "coffee," we received numbers. My number was 92693, and henceforth I was never to be called by my own name, but must respond only to this number. My father received number 92692. Once again we were lucky that the Germans did not realize we were father and son. Had they done so, one or both of us would have been killed immediately. We always tried to stay together, and included my cousin Mottel in our pact.

Now that we had numbers, we had to wait for further developments. Once again we stood in line for another roll call, and a few ss looked us over from top to bottom. We wondered what they were looking for, until one German spotted a man wearing his own shoes instead of the wooden sabots we had been issued. He was forced to take off his shoes, and the German officer ripped them apart. He found gold and diamonds hidden in the shoes and the man was shot right on the spot in front of our eyes. Once again we were saved from death; my father's hernia belt was hidden, while this man's shoes were visible to the Gestapo officer.

Once again we stood in line, this time for lunch. Around noontime we were served watery soup, and in the evening we got thin soup with a chunk of bread. We would wolf down the food, trying to assuage our hunger pains long enough to fall asleep. Since bread was the principal currency of the camp, all prisoners were emaciated, reduced to about one third of their former weight, trying to save a portion of the meager bread ration for trading.

My father worried about his hernia belt because he had sewn gold and diamonds into it. Since bread was the camp currency, he planned that we would trade gold for bread, but for the first few days we did nothing but explore our new surroundings.

I found that the camp had a number of barracks, an electrified fence, watchtowers, and crematoria. There were many different people. We Jews were considered the lowest caste. Most of the prisoners were non-Jews, Greek, English, and American POWs, political prisoners and Poles, Russians, French, Yugoslavs, and others; most were criminals, murderers. I was told that the camp had been built only a few years earlier (1940), and every barrack was made of wood from the trees that had been cut down in the forest by human sweat and blood. Only manual labor was used; the same system was still in place.

Each group was segregated from the others by fences; the women were also separated from the men by a fence. We were forbidden to communicate with people in any area other than our own, and were punished for failure to obey. Punishments were given frequently, often for no reason. Guards and kapos carried truncheons and used them freely. Tower guards had orders to shoot any prisoner who approached too close to the fence, or who was out of line, or who spoke during roll call or within three feet of an ss officer. In the principal form of punishment (other than hanging), the unfortunate prisoner was tied to a table, and twenty or forty lashes with an ox whip were applied to his buttocks in front of a few thousand of his fellow inmates. We prisoners had to count the lashes from the start to the finish, including the prisoner being punished. If the victim lost count, the count began again from the beginning. Then the open wounds were treated with iodine, and he was ordered to do several deep knee bends to prove himself fit for work. If he could not satisfy our captors that he was still fit, he would be killed immediately.

Despite the starvation, the dawn-to-dusk workday, and the ceaseless harassment, we did not lose our will to live. The first few days in camp were spent trying to keep warm. We stood outside the barracks in the cold to get some sun. We huddled very closely together to conserve body heat. After a while the people closest to the center came out and the people on the outer edges went into the center to warm up. In this way we formed a human oven and managed to survive the freezing temperature.

My father became acquainted with a Polish prisoner who seemed to have plenty of food, especially bread. My father promised him gold for five loaves of bread. The trade was to start with one loaf, which was to be passed through the fence. The first loaf came through without problems, but it was the first and last time. We never saw him again. The gold was gone, and the Pole was gone. We could not complain that we had been tricked because we would have been in trouble for trading through the fence with someone from the other side. So that was the end of that. Every time we did business, our lives were in jeopardy.

Now the question was what to do with the support belt that we had ripped apart to take out the gold. We threw away the belt after removing the rest of the gold and diamonds. Now we had to devise a new hiding place. My father decided to take apart the shaving brush, which had a hollow bottom, and hide the treasure there.

The brush and the rest of our belongings were hidden in the pouch that my father had made for me. I carried it with me every minute of the day, and made sure that no one saw it except my father and cousin. When the day was over, and we were ready to go to bed, there was a rush to the barracks to get a top or middle tier on the bed, because those on the bottom tier had to sleep four across. The first week was unbearable, with very little food or sleep.

Each day of our second week, the Nazis called out twenty people to be assigned to a work crew. We were not sure if the twenty people were more fortunate than we were; we were jealous that at least they got the chance to get out of this rotten hole for a while. As it turned out, the work crew was taken to the forest to carry logs on their shoulders. They worked under a kapo who had been a murderer on the outside; he became a kapo so that he could still kill people, this time under orders from the Nazi supervisor. After the workday was over, only eighteen people came back. The prisoners, in groups of eight or ten, had to carry logs through the forest. One man was taller than the others so he had to bend down to carry it. The kapo hit the prisoner over the head, knocked him down, and beat him until he died. The other man had his brains knocked out. The bodies were left in the forest. These episodes were common because the kapo had orders to eliminate as many Jews as he could, and he enjoyed his assignment.

The next day twenty more men were called out to work in the forest. A man whose number was called had no choice; he had to go and hope he would not be killed. We were never sure if a person who went out in the morning would come back at night. We had to live with this knowledge and try to stay alive.

Some days we worked in the camp, pushing wagons that usually were hitched to a four-horse team. Six men pulled from the front and six pushed each side and the back. Some wagons were heavier than others, depending on the load: wood, potatoes, clothing, shoes, human hair, eyeglasses, etc. Every day Jews arrived in this notorious concentration camp, some to suffer and some to die and be destroyed in the crematoria. Their belongings ended up in the wagons, and were sorted, some sent away to be used by the German population and some put into storage in warehouses.

Every day we had roll call, sometimes twice a day. Every time they counted us, there were fewer and fewer inmates. Some couldn't take the torture any more, and walked into the electrified fence to be killed either by the electricity or by the guards on the watchtowers.

Sick people were not permitted to stay in the barracks; they were immediately taken to the crematoria if they couldn't work.

I was lucky to stay well for four weeks, but I was sick in the fifth week. I went to roll call nevertheless, and worked all day.

One night I had such high fever that I felt I was burning up. I slept very fitfully, waking often to get a drink of water. Suddenly I realized that something was missing from my neck—the little pouch my father had made! All my possessions were gone! I searched all night to no avail. All our gold and diamonds were gone. I could not be sure who had taken it, but I had my suspicions. I couldn't accuse anyone unless I was sure of his guilt, so I questioned many prisoners, but no one could help me. I couldn't sleep for the rest of the night.

Although I was burning with fever, I knew that if I reported myself sick it would mean the end of me. I found my cousin to tell him of my loss, and together we searched for my father in the dark of the night. We had to tell him also before the workday began because after roll call I wouldn't see him all day.

We lined up for *Appell* together, my cousin on one side of my father, and I on the other. Before the Nazis began calling our numbers, I quickly told my father what had happened to me in the middle of the night. He fainted and began to sink to the ground. My cousin and I held him up, and, for the first and only time in my life, I slapped my father's face so he would come to himself. Thank God, by the time the numbers were called, he was conscious again and could answer to his number, otherwise we would have been killed. We felt it was really a miracle that we survived this ordeal.

Although we asked for information from the people among whom I had slept, no one would admit anything. The outcome was that we were left with nothing except my father's golden teeth that were still in his mouth, and the silver ring on my finger.

The day my possessions were stolen was the darkest day of our lives, but people shouldn't give up on life quickly. We decided that there was hope, and we would live through this as we had lived through everything else till now. Sure enough, we never gave up hope in God and He helped us. From that day on, things started getting better for us.

In a way, we felt it had been for the best that our possessions were stolen. If we had been caught with gold and diamonds, we would have been shot immediately. My father planned to sell his golden teeth if necessary, and I still had my silver ring, but we heard rumors that we would soon be moved out of Stutthof, and we stopped trading.

Although most days we were taken out of the camp to work in the forest or did manual labor in the camp, some days we just stood on line for roll call for hours. We stood in the cold from morning till night; some people were screaming and crying from the tension and strain. Suddenly it would become quiet, and we knew they had died. Some days were declared holidays. On those days we did not work, but instead were forced to watch the Germans hang prisoners. For them it was entertainment, but for us it was punishment. I'll never forget that sight for the rest of my life. I see it all the time; I live with it and sleep with it.

We felt that we really had to get out of the camp, we couldn't bear this much longer. We asked everyone what could be done to get out.

The next day at roll call the Germans selected five hundred men to work in Magdeburg, a factory near Berlin. We all lined up to be chosen, but my father, Mottel, and I had no luck. They picked workers in numerical order and had enough men before they came to our numbers. Another time we heard that they were looking for mechanics, tinsmiths, and locksmiths. I convinced my father that we should tell the Germans that we were mechanics. It took three more weeks, and finally we left the concentration camp through this lie. There was no other way for us to escape; if not for that lie we would never have come out alive.

We felt that every day was a year, every second something terrible happened, and every minute we heard different news. We didn't know whom to believe and what should be done. There were no days and no nights. We were completely cut off from the world, and even from the other parts of the camp. Barbed wire, triple guards, and guard towers separated us from everything. We knew there were other types of prisoners in the camp, including women, but we were completely isolated except for our brutal kapos and a few Germans.

Every day we were in for a different unpleasant surprise. Eight weeks without a bath or a shower, eight weeks filled with plenty of lice. Eight weeks of seeing people shot, bludgeoned, hanged, and committing suicide. I'll never forget those eight weeks in Stutthof until I die. We were unwilling witnesses to all the horrors.

When I speak about my experiences during the war, I ask my audience if any of them are Holocaust survivors. Even when there are survivors in the audience, very few of them have heard of Stutthof, because very few people survived. We owe our lives to the countless miracles that protected us throughout everything we underwent.

8

DEATH MARCH

THROUGHOUT MY LIFE, I live with my memories, and they will never escape me. I am obsessed with my enemy and talk about him all the time. I always show respect for the law, but whenever I see a policeman, I am reminded of the Latvian police who collaborated with the Nazis, the ss officers who commanded the ghetto and the camps, and the Russian soldiers from whom we had to flee after liberation. Whenever I pass through metal detectors at airports, hospitals, and schools, I am reminded of the sinister gates leading to the ghetto and concentration camps.

Yes, my experiences will never escape my mind. I can never forget, how can I forgive? But I use my experiences to direct my life to help others. I have not become bitter; I always look for good in everyone. I feel a sense of satisfaction whenever I can be of help to anyone, and my slogan is, "What can I do for you today?" I feel that by helping others, I help to establish a sense of humanity in the world.

We were uneasy as we boarded the trucks that would take us out of Stutthof in December 1944. After all, these same trucks were used to transport Jews to the crematoria to be killed. We did not know where they were taking us, but at least we were out of kz Stutthof. We found out that we were on our way to the camp called Burgraben.

Burgraben was heaven compared to Stutthof: No more hangings, no more killings, no more suicides. No more sleeping in three tiers, four to a bed. No more standing in line to be counted several times each day. No more standing in line and waiting to be taken to the forest. No more standing in a huddle trying to keep warm in the icy winter weather. Stutthof was nothing less than hell on earth.

Five hundred prisoners arrived in Burgraben and were assigned to barracks with stoves and bunk beds. The first thing they did was count us and divide us into two groups of 250 men each. The first group was ordered to work a factory day shift, and the second group was assigned the night shift. We worked from December 1944 until February 1945; the Allied forces had already won, and the war was drawing to a close but our work had to go on. The Russian air force continually bombed Danzig and the factory, but we were still forced to work as if nothing had changed.

Burgraben was near Danzig and our work was in a submarine factory twenty kilometers from the camp. Unfortunately we had been assigned to the night shift, and each time we went to work, we traveled by train for two hours to reach the railroad station in Danzig, and then we walked for another hour to arrive at the factory. Our work consisted of filing metal parts all through the night.

The 250 men who worked in the daytime were lucky in their assignment. Our "night shift" really started at two in the afternoon. We had to line up to be counted so the Nazis could be sure that the full complement of workers was there to be loaded onto the cattle cars for the trip to Danzig. When we arrived at the station, the civilians would move away from us because of our appearance and odor. We were dirty and lousy, and some of us were sick, but we all had to work, since whoever couldn't work was sent back to be exterminated in Stutthof.

After our three-hour journey, we worked from 6 P.M. until 6 A.M., and then traveled another three hours back to arrive at Burgraben at 9 A.M. We slept until 2 P.M., received our daily ration, and got ready for the 3 P.M. trip back to the factory. Thus our twelve-hour shift really took nineteen hours. Many times we didn't get any sleep at all. There was work to be done in the camp, and the day shift was already on its way to the factory, so we were ordered to unload trainloads of potatoes and clean up the camp during the day.

I was the youngest in the night shift group. We filed metal parts all night long, but whenever errands had to be run, I did them. If tools were needed, the workers called on me, and I would run to the storage room for replacement equipment. Whenever I left the work area, I managed to look for food. Once I found moldy bread in a garbage can and brought it to my father. I often returned to that garbage can, outside the German kitchen, to collect the moldy bread that helped keep us alive.

The Germans decided to give us a bath to control our louse infestation. They took us to a bathhouse near Danzig, and all 250 night shift workers were bathed. It took all day, since the facility could only handle twenty-five people at a time. The bath was a simple process: twenty-five people undressed, their clothes were thrown into an oven to kill the lice, and the people showered quickly. Then the next twenty-five men were processed, and so on until everyone had been bathed.

We had to wait a full day with no food or drink. I decided to jump over a fence and look for food and found some rotten apples. We ate them until everyone had been bathed, and then it was time to go back to work. We hadn't eaten a food ration for thirty-six hours.

During the march back to the factory, one of my friends had a heart attack and died in the street. The guards simply pushed him out of the way, against the sidewalk, and we kept on marching back to work.

We worked the night shift for four weeks until the Nazis switched shifts, and we began to work days, cleaning the submarines. Eight thousand people worked in the factory: 7,500 prisoners and 500 Germans. The prisoners were from various countries, including Yugoslavia, France, Greece, Russia, Poland, the Netherlands and England, and we all worked together, but we Jews did the hardest and dirtiest work in the factory.

After we had served a few weeks on the day shift, the Russians stepped up their bombing of the factory, rails, and train station, and we couldn't go to work. We remained at the camp for several days while the local people picked us out the lineup to work for them. It was January, and some prisoners were ordered to shovel the snow off the highways, others pushed trucks and busses off the roads, and still others were assigned to clean the railroad tracks at the intersection.

Some of my friends were assigned to push stalled trucks off the road, but as they were working, the wheels slipped, the vehicles rolled backwards and my friends were crushed to death. It was a terrible scene as they lay in the bloody snow with their intestines spilling out of their bodies. The corpses were buried there at the side of the road. The Germans gambled with our lives; every day was a game of Russian roulette, and we never knew who would be the loser.

One day a railway clerk chose twenty men to work under him, and my cousin and I were included in the crew. We took shovels, picks, and crowbars and walked about twelve kilometers, clearing ice off the tracks and shoveling snow from the guard shacks on the way. We walked and worked until noon with nothing to eat or drink.

We were taken to the site of an accident where the train had been bombed, and the cars had overturned. We thought we would have a break, but a crane soon arrived, and we helped put the cars back on the tracks. This took a few hours, and we thought that when we were finished we would return to the camp. Instead the guard decided that we should continue to clean the tracks. It was dark, and we were tired and hungry, but we had to continue working.

The twenty-man crew was divided into three groups. My friend and I noticed that one of the cars was filled with luggage, food, and cigarettes. We decided that on the way back we would take a chance with our lives and steal some of the cigarettes. If the guard questioned us about the extra time we used, we would say we had stopped to relieve ourselves on the side of the tracks. We jumped into the car, and each took a case of cigarettes, which consisted of one hundred packs. We went into the brake booth and ripped the cases apart so we could hide the small packs in our trousers. We were lucky that the guard did not notice what we were doing.

As soon as the column of men reached us, we fell right into line with the rest of the men, tired, wet, and dirty. Getting through the gate without being discovered with the cigarettes was a matter of life or death, but by carrying a pick and shovel I did not look conspicuous. When we arrived at camp at nine P.M., I was so happy and excited that I was not hungry. With cigarettes, our future looked better; now we had merchandise to trade for extra food, which would help us survive. I returned my tools to the shed before going to the barracks. My cousin, who was with us on the work crew, had managed to grab three packs of cigarettes without my knowledge and returned to the barracks before me.

My father was very excited about the three packs my cousin gave him; it was as if he had been given gold. He asked my cousin if I had also found cigarettes, but Mottel didn't know. I walked into the barracks a short time later, climbed into bed, and began stowing my one hundred packs of cigarettes into a bag. My father and my cousin could not believe their eyes.

Within half an hour, we received an order that the twenty men who had worked near that train car should report immediately to the commandant's office. Obviously the Nazis had realized that cigarettes were missing, and it was clear to me that others had also taken advantage of the open train car to steal some of the cases. Before reporting to the commandant, I instructed my father to stash the cigarettes with a friend in case of an inspection.

First we received a good beating from the kapo, and then they interrogated us. Since everyone said that he had only two or three packs, I said the same. Some claimed to have had only one pack, and even that one had been lost in the latrine, which was an open pit. All of us had to surrender the cigarettes we held. Although we prisoners were punished for stealing, the next day the kapo and his henchmen went with volunteers to join the conductor in looting the train.

When my father went back to his friend to take back our cigarettes, half of them were already gone, but there was nothing we could do about it. At least we still had the rest of the bundle, and it was very valuable. For three cigarettes we could get a pair of shoes; for five, a jacket; for two, a loaf of bread. We were rich, but not without having taken a chance with our lives. Again we escaped death by the firing squad.

We Jews did not leave the camp again until the camp closed near the end of January 1945, but additional prisoners from other camps were brought in. They were well dressed and well fed, and we traded our cigarettes for their bread. Before I stole the cigarettes, things had been very bad in the camp because we had almost nothing left to trade. Although I had my sterling silver ring fashioned from the last teaspoon of my parents' set by the goldsmith Isser Lurie in the Riga ghetto, I couldn't bring myself to sell it. At that time I considered it my talisman, and I still do. It was more precious to me than anything else, and in a very irrational way I believed it brought us luck.

At one time my father decided to trade his gold teeth for bread. His friend, a dentist, pulled out the teeth with a pair of pliers. My father was very disappointed, however, since all he got for the teeth was a half-loaf of bread. After that, we had nothing more to trade until I stole those cigarettes. The teeth had been our last resort, but we learned never to give up hope. Now we had a valuable commodity to trade with. Even on the subsequent death march in early February 1945, we traded those cigarettes until we had no more.

Close to five hundred of us still lived. We were ordered out of the camp and began to march. During the death march, we slept in many different places, in barracks, stables, churches, camps, and, despite the cold, even under the open sky. Every morning we were counted, and if someone was missing we had to wait in line until he was found, either dead or alive. If alive, he was either stabbed with a bayonet or shot, in order to discourage us from trying to escape. But most of the time, the missing prisoner had already died of cold or fatigue.

On the way we came across German army marching units, running in the opposite direction. We could tell from their faces that the war was over, and they were running from the victorious Russian army. However, the ss never gave up. They continued the march and shot those of us who could not walk any farther.

The last night of the march, we stopped at a prison camp, and the ss guards, tired of herding us around, wanted to leave us there. The camp commandant accepted only about half of the remaining Jews, stating that the camp could not hold any more. We were very disappointed; we wanted to stop marching already. However, the camp was infected with typhus, and those "lucky" prisoners who were placed there soon contracted the fatal illness. Once again, we were saved, this time because we had been marching in the second half of the line.

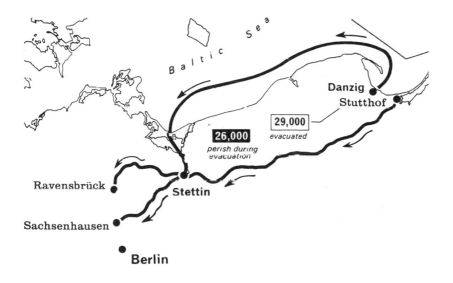

Route of the Death March from Stutthof to Stettin, February, 1945

9

THE RUSSIANS ARRIVE

FINALLY WE REACHED A CAMP called Gottsdorf. We were counted and found we had lost two hundred men on the death march. Only about three hundred of us had survived, my father and I among them. In Gottsdorf there was a mixture of prisoners, men and women. The barracks did not have beds, only shelves, but the dead prisoners had left us a legacy of lice, which ate us up alive. We were busy all day and all night killing our enemies, the vermin.

We had become accustomed to a variety of accommodations by this time. We had experienced so many beds in the years of the German occupation! When we had arrived in the ghetto, our apartment was small, and sleeping was a bit uncomfortable. My brothers and I slept two in a bed because the apartment had only two bedrooms, one of which we had given to the German Jewish couple we had taken in. When we were chased into the small ghetto, ten men slept in one apartment, and I shared a bed with my father. Those beds had no pillowcases or sheets; in any case, there were no facilities to wash linens. Our next sleeping quarters, in Lenta, utilized bunk beds. My father slept on the bottom tier, and I took the top. We had pillows and mattresses stuffed with straw, but when you are young and work hard all day, you can sleep almost anywhere.

Our first experience with sleeping outside came at Salaspils. No pillow, no mattress, just you, yourself, with your arm to cushion your head. On our voyage across the Baltic Sea, we slept in each other's arms. On the barges up the Vistula, we didn't sleep at all; we were forced to stand for a day and a night until we reached Stutthof.

In Stutthof itself, there were three-tiered bunks, packed with ten people, four on the bottom and three on the middle and top tiers. On the death march, we slept anywhere, in stables, barns, and outdoors. In Burgraben, there were bunks like those in Lenta.

In Gottsdorf, there were no beds; the barrack consisted of a potbellied stove and two tiers of shelves, where human beings were stacked like merchandise. We shared everything we had, the food, the heat, the lice, the filth, and the sickness.

Gottsdorf was not a labor camp, but some people did work in the forest, and I had a job in the kitchen. I cut wood for the cooking fire, dug potatoes from the pits where they were stored, and brought them to the kitchen.

One day when I brought potatoes to the kitchen, I put a few into my pants, which fit me loosely and were tied around the ankles as well as held on by a rope belt. The ss guard spotted me; he ordered me to take out the potatoes and lie down on a bench. I had to lift up my coat and he began to whip me. I had to count the blows until he reached twenty-five, but I was in so much pain I skipped a few numbers, and the guard forced me to start again from the beginning, while my father watched, aghast. Thank God I was young and strong; it was a miracle that I survived that beating and was able to go to roll call that night.

A few days later I decided to steal potatoes again from the same pit. I sneaked out of the barracks at night so the guard wouldn't see me. The potato pit was at the bottom of the hill and I ran quietly down. I filled up my pants and started climbing back up the hill, but I rustled the bushes as I passed and suddenly, machine gun fire burst all around me. Luckily, I ducked and the bullets missed.

I ran as fast as I could to the barrack and dived into bed. The sound of the shooting woke everyone up, and my father asked me at whom they were shooting. I didn't want him to worry, so I said I didn't know. They shot somebody or something every day and every night anyway.

One day we went to the forest to collect wood for the kitchen, and we found a dead horse. We brought in the meat along with the wood; I cut up the meat and hid it in a broken-down car, intending to give it to the cook the next day. But the next day it was gone; someone else had taken it.

Many days we had very little to eat. The ss guards knew we didn't have enough food and used our hunger to amuse themselves. They would throw vegetables into the middle of a field and watch as the women fought over the food. The kitchen was very tiny, and the camp was so crowded that everything had to be cooked in two shifts. They never peeled the potatoes, just threw them in the pot covered with dirt, so the potato soup was full of sand. We had no meat, except for the second dead horse I discovered by accident. This time I was smart enough to cook it right away.

I organized some people, including a few women, and we became partners in the meat. The women cooked it and my friend Edelstein had salt. When the meat had finished cooking, we all sat down to eat a good meal for a change. The cooking utensils were very simple, just bricks and cinder blocks for a fireplace and a discarded five-gallon metal can for a cooking pot. The fire performed two functions: not only did it cook the meat, but also gave the women a chance to warm up.

Sometimes people tried to escape from the camp, but were usually recaptured. After they were brought back to camp, the ss tied them to a tree, and we prisoners had to whip them and beat them with sticks until they died. If we refused, we ourselves would be whipped to death. We had to take the bodies deep into the forest for burial. This happened often, because the prisoners took hope from the fact that the Russian army was approaching, and thought that if they could escape, the Russians would liberate them. Half of the escapees had no luck; they were caught and tortured to death.

I'll never forget what happened to Mr. Leiberman. He was a good, experienced electrician; we had been together in Lenta. We had gone through Stutthof, Burgraben, and the death march together, and now we were at the end of our rope in Gottsdorf. I saw Mr. Leiberman being dragged on the ground by one of the kapos, half-dead, with his brains knocked out by the kapo's cudgel. I don't know what he had done to receive such a punishment, but he was thrown into a pit not far from the potato pits. The ss wanted to show the other prisoners what can happen to a human being in one moment. He wasn't shot, but even a piece of metal pipe can kill, and he died in the pit.

The few weeks we were in the camp were chaotic. No food was delivered, so we had to live on potatoes, some vegetables, and a few dead horses. Every day we had to bury the prisoners who had died overnight. Additional prisoners came from different camps, some of which had been liquidated by the Germans. They marched the remaining prisoners to Gottsdorf, where they slept on the ground outside the barracks, fully dressed, in the freezing winter.

We knew the end was near, but the big question was how it would come. All the guards were nervous, and the Germans couldn't decide what to do with so many prisoners and so few guards. Their decision came one night, when everyone who was capable of walking was assembled outside in the courtyard in the middle of the camp and told to be ready to leave. My father felt that he would not survive another march. He formulated a plan that we followed to the letter. He stood on the line with my cousin and me and as soon as the march started we walked with the group until the gate and then made a left turn toward the barracks. The guards didn't see us, and we disappeared in the dark. Once again, we took a chance with our lives and survived.

We had made the right decision, for luck was with us. That very morning, March 10, 1945, the Russians arrived to liberate the camp. All night long we had hidden in the barracks. We found out that the head of the camp and all his henchmen were also hiding from the Russians. We heard the sound of a Russian tank, and then a shell exploded in the kitchen barrack. Only one kapo was inside, an Austrian Jew named Shorr. When he saw the Russians coming, he ran into the barrack, waving his arms over his head. The Russians had seen someone moving, and not knowing he was a prisoner, blew up the kitchen barrack with him inside. Shorr was in the wrong place at the wrong time, and his luck had run out.

Within minutes we saw Russian soldiers running through the camp, searching for the ss and other German soldiers. The German guards wanted to outsmart the Russians, so they took off their uniforms and put on prisoner uniforms or civilian clothes. It was a situation of every man for himself. Most of the prisoners who had remained in camp were old or sick and had been told they would be shot because they hadn't gone on the march. We had taken the chance of staying behind, knowing that by staying with the German guards one more day we might be shot. Our luck was with us again, and instead we were liberated in the morning.

The Allied armies had different styles of liberation. The inmates of those camps that were liberated by the Americans were immediately quarantined in the camps to reduce the spread of typhus and given food and medical treatment. The freed prisoners were often assisted in relocating and helped to find jobs. Camps liberated by the English fared equally well. In fact, many young people liberated by the British, such as Elie Wiesel, were educated and trained by the liberators.

How different from liberation by the Russian army! As soon as the Russians had eliminated our German guards, we were left completely on our own. We were not given food or medical care, and had to fend for ourselves in the German countryside.

We were all free, but we did not know what to do or where to go. Many of us, although no longer prisoners, were still sick. I was relatively healthy, however, so I "liberated" a horse and wagon, brought it to the camp, and loaded it with sick people. There were more people than would fit on one wagon, so we commandeered more wagons and horses from the German civilians, who fled from the approaching Russian army. Relatively healthy former prisoners drove our caravan of sick Jews to the hospital.

My father, cousin, a few friends, and I decided to walk from the camp to a small town named Lauenburg. On the way I saw a wagon loaded with food, mostly bread. I filled a bag, stuffed it into a potato sack, and put it on a bicycle. I pushed the bike, and we walked on.

Coming toward us were Russian soldiers marching toward the city of Stettin. We saw long columns of German civilians and long columns of Russian soldiers. They stopped us many times and questioned us. As they asked us who we were, I noticed guards from Gottsdorf wearing civilian clothes and prisoner's uniforms, hiding in the crowd, trying to save their lives. We spoke to the Soviet soldiers in Russian and told them that German guards and ss officers were disguised among the refugees. The Russians shot them on the spot as we pointed them out.

A German Jewish doctor had been with me in various camps where he had helped the ss, still proud of being a German. Now he walked close to us, hoping that we would hide him. We couldn't help him; he had collaborated with the ss and the Russians considered him a Nazi. The Russian soldiers shot him also.

Another German Jew had been the chief of police in a different camp and had acted just like the doctor. His fellow prisoners had drowned him in a pit full of human waste. They pushed him under the surface time after time as he screamed for help, until he finally died. Somehow, people don't forget what was done to them, and they bide their time until they can take revenge.

When we reached Lauenburg (now Lebork, Poland), on the night of March 10, 1945, we were still on our own, unlike the Jews who remained in DP camps, fed,and treated by the British and Americans.

We found an abandoned apartment. We took off our filthy prisoner uniforms and indulged in the luxury of bathing. Our clothing was full of lice, and we couldn't bear to put it on again, so we found civilian clothes in the apartment and got dressed. We decided to search for food in the morning.

I found jars of cherry preserves and some other food in a pantry and cooked breakfast. My father, my cousin, and I left the apartment to look for more food even though we still had some of the bread that I had loaded on the bicycle the day before liberation. We separated to search for butter, bacon, or chicken in other apartments in our new neighborhood. Mottel and I returned to the apartment, but my father was caught by Russian soldiers and taken away. I waited and waited all day, listening to the shooting that went on continuously as the Russians fought the Germans whose resistance was unbelievably desperate.

I was worried all day; I thought that my father had been killed by the Germans or Russians in the crossfire. When he finally walked into the apartment at twilight, we felt like it was a holiday. We asked what had happened to him, and he explained that because he had been wearing civilian clothes, the

Russians took him for a spy. He spoke to them in Russian, but that made the matter worse. The Russians accused him of being a German sent to spy on Russia. He protested and said that he was Jewish, but the Russians asked, "How could a Jew remain alive since Hitler killed off all the Jews?"

They thought his story was very suspicious and took him with them to be examined by a superior officer. As luck would have it, they took him to a very high-ranking officer, a general in the Russian army, because they were sure they had caught an important spy. The general told his soldiers, "I'll take care of this spy." It turned out that the general was Jewish, and my father spoke to him in Yiddish. He explained that he had been liberated the previous day with his son, had been looking for food and had been caught in the net. It was just like the Bible story when Joseph was viceroy in Egypt and his brothers didn't recognize him. He was one of them, and he saved them, just as the general, a Jew like us, saved my father. It was history repeating itself.

My father returned to the apartment, without food but safe. The general gave him strict orders that all of us should lie low in the apartment for at least a week, and then send someone out to see if the situation is safe, just like in the Bible story of Noah and the dove.

We finally found something to eat. I was the cook and concocted a carrot, potato, and bacon pudding that we devoured like starving people. Six men lived in the apartment, and in a few days everyone became ill with typhus. We were all very thirsty and had stomach pains, but none of us could leave the apartment even if we had wanted to. Somehow the one who was least sick managed to arrange a horse and wagon to take us to the hospital and that was the last we saw of the apartment for several months.

I was as one dead; I didn't remember anything that had happened to my father or me since I became sick. I was so delirious

I didn't even remember going to the hospital. For a week I slept in the same bed as my father without knowing it. There was such a shortage of beds that the patients slept two in a bed and even on the floor in the hallways and the rooms. They brought patients in by the thousands, and even the nurses and the doctors were sick. Barbers shaved the heads and bodies of the patients because hair harbored the lice that carried the disease.

It was chaos. Men and women alike were chained to their beds and put into straitjackets because of their delirium. I myself believed that I had seven holes in my head, that my head was twisted, and that I needed a brain operation. I kept searching for a cool spot to sleep in, and finally found one under the bed. After I came to myself I looked for my father and was amazed to discover that he was right beside me. Miraculously we had stayed together even in our illness.

After a few weeks I began to improve, and started to walk around the hospital, looking into the various rooms. I found a friend of mine, but when I went back to see him a second time, he was gone. He had jumped out of the window after telling the other patients that he saw his mother through the window. He jumped out to be with her, and that was the end of him.

Some people, especially women, were tied to their beds with handcuffs. They looked terrible, with shaven heads. Everywhere we saw young beautiful girls whose looks were spoiled by their shaven heads. We had no desire for them; they were sick, skinny, and bald, but after a few months their looks improved. The same could be said for the men. We were in the hospital for two months, from approximately March 13 until May 15, 1945. My father was with me all the time.

While we were in the hospital, a Russian captain who was not sick walked around and questioned us. He wanted to know our names, where we were from, our professions, our country, our nationality but not our religion. As atheists the Russians were not concerned with religion, and this officer was from the NKVD, the secret police. The outcome was simple; after we recovered the officer gave us work assignments.

The day I was declared cured of typhus I became a watchman with a rifle, and set as a guard at the gate of the hospital. This was my job from May 15 to July 15, 1945. The hospital workers were local Germans, Russian nurses, and German nurses. I spoke both Russian and German, and could converse with them in their respective languages.

There was not much to do in Lauenburg; there were no theaters or cinemas. All one could do for entertainment was go to parties to drink and meet women, then leave the party to have sex. I met a German-Jewish girl who was pregnant. I asked her who the father was, and she said, "The barber."

The hospital employed a Russian soldier to shave the patients' heads to prevent a lice epidemic, and he enjoyed the favors of several young girls whom he made pregnant. Each survivor who left Lauenburg after the summer took a package along. These girls carried away with them their Russian babies.

Most of the women and girls I met in Lauenburg were from Poland, German, Italy, France, Lithuania, Czechoslovakia, and Austria, but not Latvia. Almost all of the Latvian women had been killed in 1941.

After my father became well, the captain put him to work as a tailor. He set up shop with some other workers. My father took a soldier with him, and they searched through Lauenburg for sewing machines. When they found a few machines, they set up shop and housekeeping in a house near the hospital. My father had another tailor, A. Hoffman, to work with him. Hoffman was an undiscriminating womanizer. He slept with anyone he could, whether German or Jewish girls. He lived up to his reputation until he contracted syphilis. He confided in me and trusted me to find him a doctor. I found a doctor who prescribed a salve to heal Hoffman's rash.

Hoffman asked two girls who were seamstresses to work for them when the girls were ready to leave the hospital. In the shop they made new uniforms for the army and did some repair work. The two girls were young and beautiful sisters who had come from Hungary. They worked in the shop until July, and then they decided to go back to Hungary, but they had a big problem.

They were young and beautiful and spoke only German and Hungarian; it was dangerous for them to go out alone. The Russian soldiers frequently attacked the local German girls, raping them all night. Women were afraid to go out into the streets because if the Russians caught them, they were taken to the barracks and forced to have sex with twenty or twenty-five soldiers.

I decided to help the girls get back to their home. The question was where and how to take them in those dangerous times.

During our stay in Lauenburg we came into contact with Jews from different cities. Some came from as far as Lodz, Poland. They brought food to sell, transporting it by horse and wagon or by train. The peddlers from Lodz, especially, brought us information about the world outside Lauenburg.

They told us that no one should return to Riga, because those who tried were stopped by the border guards and sent to Siberia to work in the labor camps.

I suggested to my father that I would take the girls to Lodz and come back with enough information to make the decision where we should go ourselves. I promised the girls that I would take them, posing as their brother. They agreed to my plan, and we planned the train trip for the twenty-four-hour journey from Lauenburg to Lodz. They had to be mute for the whole trip so as not to betray their true origin, and I was to be their spokesman.

During our last days in the apartment, we packed everything and then left for the railroad station. We waited three hours for the train to arrive from Stettin; it was packed to the roof with people, who even hung onto the roof. We managed to get in, and we were off to Lodz. The Russian soldiers questioned everyone all over again: Where were we from? Where were we going? I spoke for the sisters and myself. We trembled with fear until they accepted our answers because the soldiers found some people whose answers they didn't like and took them away. Finally, after a full day's journey, we arrived in the city of Lodz.

Lodz was very different from Lauenburg. There was an information center in the middle of the city, and people came to the center to inquire for relatives and to leave information about themselves in case anyone came to ask about them. Some people were able to reunite with their relatives and to plan for the future. They had to decide whether to go home or to find a new homeland.

The two sisters decided to go back to Hungary, so after three days in Lodz I took them to the train station. I said goodbye to them there and never saw them again. I decided to return to Lauenburg to rejoin my father.

When I came back to the apartment, I found a big surprise. The Russian captain from the NKVD was waiting for me, and his first words were, "Where have you been? I've been looking for you. I have a very important job for you."

I had been working as a watchman at the hospital gate, keeping an eye on the German workers as they entered and left the hospital. Now the captain recommended me for a new job; he wanted me to become an informer for the secret police.

I went to the police station, where I watched how the NKVD tortured people in the basement. I met a German Jew who had been liberated a few months earlier from a concentration camp. He was being tortured because he did not speak Russian, and they thought that he was a spy. He was lucky that I had come at the right time. I spoke to the captain and explained that this man was not a Nazi but a German Jew with whom I had been in concentration camps. I vouched for him, and thanks to me he remained alive.

Various NKVD people interviewed me, and they all gave me instructions in what I was to do and how I must behave as a German. I spent a full day at the police station, and when I returned home in the evening, I had not yet given them an answer. They wanted me to commit myself to join them, but I explained that I had to discuss the issue with my father. I asked for some time to think, but they claimed they needed my services right away. German snipers were still shooting Russian soldiers, and they wanted to find out who was involved.

Since I spoke German and Russian fluently, they wanted me to act as a spy and counterspy. This left me between two fires—I could be killed by the Germans or the Russians, whichever side thought I was betraying them. I knew I had to be very careful, and after a full discussion with my father, I came to one conclusion. We had to disappear from the city of Lauenburg.

10

ESCAPE TO THE WEST

A FEW HOURS AFTER WE MADE THE DECISION, we left Lauenburg in the middle of the night. When I had taken the girls to Lodz, I had papers, which permitted them to travel with me. I never turned in those papers, and now I changed the names on them so that my father and I could use them to escape from Lauenburg. I prayed that no one would examine them too carefully, and once again we were in luck.

With just a few pieces of luggage and our falsified papers, my father and I went to the railroad station and jumped on a train. We were terrified of being arrested for our forged papers, but luck was with us and no one questioned us.

We traveled for twenty-four hours until we arrived in Lodz, and I contacted the same people we had dealt with before. They arranged for us to share an apartment, and we stayed in Lodz for two months, preparing for the next step of our journey. It was just before the High Holidays, and we planned to leave after the holidays. We changed apartments and got ready to travel again. This time our trip would not be so risky, because it was arranged by Aliyah Bet, an illegal Zionist organization which helped refugees without documents leave the Russian sphere of influence and escape to the American zone. Final destinations could be anywhere in the free world, not only Palestine. We paid our money, were assigned to a group of people, and were given a date and time to meet.

We were introduced to the people in our group and given our instructions. We were told when and where to meet for the next leg of our journey. The group consisted of men and women, single and married, young and middle-aged. We all slept in an apartment with a few rooms and not enough beds, and plenty of sharing went on. I remember we had a doctor who had deserted from the Russian army, and we obtained civilian clothes for him. He was a young man and made out very well with the ladies during our stay in the apartment. We remained in Lodz for several weeks, waiting to be assigned a guide to our unknown destination.

One night the leader of the Aliyah Bet came to our apartment, instructing us to meet at a certain time and place. We followed the leader to a hideout and were disguised as Romanians, and were issued false papers.

As we tried to board the train, we were suspected and questioned by Russian soldiers. We had been told to speak only Hebrew, and if we didn't know conversational Hebrew, we were told to recite Hebrew prayers. When the soldiers questioned us, we acted as if we didn't speak Russian, and one man recited Kaddish, that being the only Hebrew he could remember from the time that he was a young man in a little shtetl. To the Russian soldiers, Hebrew and Romanian sounded the same, so we got away.

That same day we arrived in the city of Kattowitz (now Katowice, Poland), where everything had been prepared for us. We were told we would remain there for a few days, but then we heard bad news. The Russians had gotten wind of us and were searching for refugees in the streets as well as in certain suspected spots. We had no choice but to remain in the apartment for two weeks without stepping outside until the air was clear.

Meanwhile, we became acquainted with the people in our new group. My father met Dora Glickson, a woman in our group, and he decided to marry her as soon as time would permit. As luck would have it, however, we were divided into parties of ten, and the woman remained with the other group.

Our group left Kattowitz first, again without knowing our destination. Once again we were told to speak Hebrew; this time we were disguised as Greeks with berets and pipes. We were told that we had to be very careful; this was an experimental route and our success would determine if it would be used again.

The next city was Bratislava, Slovakia. We now had to pass the Polish border, and we had to think of a way to hide our valuables. The Russian doctor made a false cast for one of our women, which we felt would pass muster with the Polish or Russian guards. He placed all our valuables and suspicious papers inside the cast and she was the first one we sent through the border control. She went through with no problem, and she wore the cast until we arrived in Germany. We told the guard that we wanted to go to Greece, and he gave us directions and told us which train to take.

We knew that the train to Bratislava would be going in the opposite direction, but we had to wait on the wrong platform as he instructed to reduce suspicion. The Bratislava train was a freight train, and would not stop in the station, but only slow down. We had to be on the alert to leap onto it as it passed through. We opened the door and rushed onto the train with all our packages, helping the women get aboard. We were on the run in the middle of the night, just like animals, but we succeeded.

We arrived in Bratislava in the morning. Some members of the group were still on the trains at the railway station, and some of them were already waiting for us in Bratislava. It was a challenge that we overcame, and a miracle that we survived.

Once again we lived in an apartment that had been assigned to us. I went to the movies with someone; we had begun to feel like free people, able to do what we wanted. But it was only an illusion; we were still waiting for instructions regarding our next move. We heard rumors that we would be going to Vienna to the Rothschilds' Hospital, which had been converted to a hostel for the refugees of Aliyah Bet.

Our new disguise was that of German Jews going to Germany. We felt good leaving Bratislava, as we were finally leaving the Russian sphere of influence. Vienna was divided into four parts, Russian, French, English, and American, and the Rothschilds' Hospital was in the American Zone.

We received new papers and new clothing and had to walk a long way, finally crossing a bridge from the Russian Zone to the American Zone. Once again people were waiting for us and took us to the hospital. It was full of people from different places who had been waiting for enough people to make up groups for their destinations. Some people had waited for a day, some for a month.

Again my father was lucky and was reunited with Dora Glickson, the lady he had left behind in Kattowitz. The atmosphere in Vienna in the Rothschilds' Hospital was wonderful. Everybody was happy, out of hiding and unafraid that any minute we could be caught and sent to jail or to Siberia.

We knew that such things did happen. Many years later, in the United States, we met a man whose son had been lost in the shuffle; they had crossed paths while traveling and looked for each other until the son wound up in Russia and the father in America. The son was later convicted of illegal activities and sent to Siberia. They were reunited in Haifa, Israel, after thirty-five years; the son had married and had children and grandchildren.

We were told to get ready for the next stage of our journey. We traveled from Vienna with happy faces and arrived in Linz, Austria, where we stayed for a few weeks. Then in September 1945, right before the High Holidays, we traveled to Munich, Germany. Some people were sent to boarding houses, but we were assigned to an apartment owned by an old German couple.

My father and I were still together, but I was unhappy doing nothing. I decided to find a Displaced Persons camp where there was a school. I wanted to learn a trade so that when I left Germany I would be able to make a future for myself. I traveled to Feldafing DP Camp, but to no avail. They did not have a school, so I came back to Munich.

I told my father I had had no luck, and we decided to postpone my search for a school until after the holidays. We went to the synagogue in Munich, and during the 1945 Yom Kippur services, I again saw blood shed.

One Jewish man recognized another as the kapo who had killed his brother. The men attacked him and almost killed him during the Yom Kippur services.

11

LANDSBERG
AND EMIGRATION

ONE OF MY FIRST SPEAKING ENGAGEMENTS in the United States was at Stern College. I was invited to speak by a history professor at the college, whom I met at a hotel where Doris and I spent a weekend. The professor was scheduled to give a lecture on Shabbat afternoon, and he spoke about Jewish history, especially about the *She'eris HaPelayta*, the "Remaining Remnants," as he referred to the Holocaust survivors, who had lived in DP camps in the American Zone in Austria and Germany from 1945–1950.

I had spent two years in the DP camp in Landsberg am Lech, while I attended the ORT school. It wasn't all work, though. We had a social life, even played sports; I joined the basketball team, and we played in tournaments with other DP camps.

The professor spoke about the effect of religion in the camps, but he was disappointed when I told him that in my opinion, the majority of the survivors were not religious.

He spoke about *sheluchim*, messengers from Palestine, agents of the Aliyah Bet, who visited the camps to recruit *olim*, new immigrants to move to Eretz Yisroel. They did not emphasize the religious life of Israel, but stressed the Zionist ideal of a Jewish homeland. He said that one of the important men who had traveled to the camps was David Ben-Gurion. I raised my hand, and the professor asked if I had a question. I said, "I was there."

The professor was shocked to see a man who had spent some time with Ben-Gurion in the DP camps. I told him that I had spoken to Ben-Gurion when he came to Landsberg.

The professor invited me to be a guest speaker to talk about the Holocaust at Stern College. The students had many, quite tough questions for me, but I believe that I gave them the right answers.

Some time ago, I again met three ladies whom I had known in Landsberg: Feigele, Mina, and Miriam. We had been good friends then, and our friendships have been rekindled.

Feigele Zimmerman married and is now Zipora Luchawitzky. She lived on a kibbutz in Germany and had a daughter, whom she named Sara, and Mina married Pina Chorofsky. All "my" three ladies are married; two of them relocated to the United States. Miriam Katz and her husband opened a grocery store, and later a supermarket.

I was already married when Mina came to the States with her son, Max, leaving Pina behind in Germany because at the time he was not well enough to travel. (He did come later.) I visited her and her son on Debevoise Street in Brooklyn. She was happy to see me, and in the summer I arranged for her to stay with my in-laws at their summer place in the mountains.

A few months later, Pina arrived, and he and Mina took an apartment in Brooklyn. A few years later, their daughter Beverly was born. Doris and I also had two children by then, Tevey and Judy.

I always kept in touch with Mina and Miriam in the States, and when my stepmother decided to go to Israel by ship in 1952, I made up a Care package for Feigele. She was now called

Zipora (Feigele is Yiddish and Zipora Hebrew for the same word: "bird"), and had two children, Sara and Joseph. They lived in Lod under terrible conditions. Zipora later told me that the package had lasted for six months.

All four of us "Litvaks" kept in touch, and when it was time to make the Bar Mitzvah for our younger son, we planned a ceremony at the Kotel. Doris and I had taken the children on an Emunah tour of Israel two years earlier, and it was my dream to see them and also to find out what had happened to my brother Mendel.

I called Zipora in Tel Aviv, and we had our first reunion in Hotel Deborah. Zipora came with her daughter and son-in-law, as well as her husband Mottel. Her son Joseph was missing; he had been killed by Arabs. My son asked if Zipora had been my girlfriend, because he knew that we had been very close, and young together without any family.

Miriam, Mina, and I always kept in touch over the years. Miriam's husband died, and a few years later she remarried, but she didn't have children with either of her husbands. Mr. Allen and Pina, both Holocaust survivors, died in recent years. Meanwhile, Doris and I made *simchas*, family celebrations. Naturally, we invited the ladies to our children's Bar Mitzvahs and weddings, as did Mina and Pina. In Israel, Zipora's daughter Sara had two children, but her husband was killed in the Arab-Israel wars. Sara remarried and had two more children, but later divorced her husband. Zipora is now a great-grandmother, but her husband Mottel passed away. Doris and I went to the wedding of one of Zipora's four grandchildren.

Mina's daughter Beverly is the controller of a big company; she is married to a lawyer and has three children. Mina's son, Professor Max Chorofsky, holds doctoral degrees in gynecology and psychiatry and treats women suffering from post-partum depression. He was married twice and has three children.

I decided that we had to have a "Litvak" reunion with my three Landsberg ladies. In 1995, Zipora came to the States alone, and stayed with Miriam, who is her cousin. Doris and I picked them up on the way to visit Mina, who lives in a nursing home in Riverdale, for the fiftieth anniversary of our liberation.

After the holidays in Munich, I heard some information about a school in Landsberg. I took a trip to the DP camp there, and was delighted to find that it had in fact an ORT-sponsored school. I registered for a course in radio mechanics and attended classes in Landsberg.

I stayed with friends while I took the course in radio technology. We lived in Block no. 5, which had three floors. Each floor had ten rooms, and each room contained ten beds. In our group four people were from Lithuania and six from Poland. The "Litvaks" stayed together in one corner of the room. Two married couples were in our group.

To preserve a semblance of privacy, we strung blankets across the room to create cubicles. Once one of the women was undressing behind her "curtain" when suddenly the blanket slipped off the rope. Nobody noticed until she screamed out in Yiddish, "Don't look at me! My blanket fell down, and I'm not dressed!"

When the Germans liquidated the Vilna ghetto in 1943–1944, they selected young women to work and murdered their relatives in the Pannar Forest. The girls were put into boxcars and shipped to the north. The first stop was Concentration Camp Kaiserwald; they were later dispersed to various work camps and ended up on the last transport from Riga to Stutthof. My father, my cousin, and I were on the same ship and the same barge, and we walked through the same gate at Stutthof, when we were separated and sent to different barracks. After liberation, we went our separate ways. Each of us had only one thing in mind—escape from the Russians.

We finally met again in the city of Lodz, Poland, where we made our preparations to leave the Russian zone with Aliyah Bet. We traveled in groups to the American Zone, and at the end of 1945, we were reintroduced to each other in Landsberg am Lech, where Hitler wrote *Mein Kampf* in 1922. We were not far from KZ Dachau and Munich, where Hitler made speeches and led demonstrations.

When we were assigned living quarters, I introduced myself, saying, "My name is Itze Ratz." The three women gave their names: Mina Rucke, Feigele Zimmerman, and Miriam Lepkowitz. We stayed together in one room with six other people: Mr. Katz, whom Miriam Lepkowitz later married; Lipmanowitz; a young blond man whom we called "Chazer Kop"; a tailor; and Mr. and Mrs. Fuchs. We four Litvaks stayed together in one corner of the room.

Miriam Lepkowitz and Mr. Katz stayed with us for only a short time; then they married and moved away. I was studying in the ORT school, Mina worked in the kitchen, and Feigele learned to be a seamstress. Feigele didn't stay in our room long; she met Mottel Luchawitzky, and they were married. Mina and I stayed together until I finished my radio mechanic course and went to Munich to study engineering.

Some of my fellow students in the Landsberg ORT school found it difficult to understand our instructor, who was German. My German was better than theirs, so I had no problem following the lessons, and invited them to study with me in our room in Block no. 5. By studying with others, I reinforced the lessons for myself, and surely helped the other students.

I traveled by train to Munich every weekend to be with my father, who lived alone during the week. I talked things over with him, and we came to an agreement. I went to visit Mrs. Glickson, the lady friend with whom we had been reunited in Vienna. She lived with her married friend. I called her and she invited us for dinner. She and I had a heart-to-heart talk, and I gave my approval for her to marry my father. They were married on December 31, 1945.

My father, his second wife, Dora, and I, shortly after their wedding in Munich, 1945

I graduated from the ORT school in May 1946 and decided to go to the Oscar von Miller Polytechnical College in Munich to study engineering. I attended college in Munich until July 1947.

Out of twenty students in the ORT class, only two of us went on to get a higher education. In order to catch up to the college students, we hired a private instructor to teach us basics of algebra and other courses, which we paid for with part of our food ration—it was really "food for thought"! I did not intend to stay in Germany for the rest of my life, and knew that my passport to the future was a profession. I was determined to learn a trade that would stand me in good stead wherever in the world I decided to live.

Graduating class of the ORT school in Landsberg; I am in the second row from the bottom, far left

Aside from my father, I had no living relatives so far as I knew, and so I was free to travel anywhere in the world, always planning to keep my father with me. Later I discovered that I had a cousin in America, and planned to go to the United States. Even though it was the middle of the school year, I felt that I could resume my studies wherever I decided to stay.

After my father's marriage, he was told to write a letter to the United States, where there was a Landsmannschaft organization in Brooklyn, New York, that helped immigrants keep in touch with their homeland. His letter wound up in the hands of a woman named Chaya Leah Silverstein, who remembered my mother's family because she had stayed in Riga during her immigration from Barafka, my father's hometown. Many people who left Russia traveled through Riga's port on their way to all parts of the world, and Mrs. Silverstein had stayed in my grandmother's house for a few months before leaving Riga for the United States. She still remembered my family.

She took my father's letter to my mother's half-brother, my Uncle Nathan, and her half-sister, my Aunt Fanny, who were overjoyed to hear that Moshe Ratz, his wife and son were still alive. (They naturally thought that their half-sister, my mother, was still alive.) My uncle's daughter Jean wrote to me in Landsberg, stating that she would do everything in her power to save her aunt and bring her out of Germany with her husband and son.

I sorrowfully wrote back, telling Jean that her aunt had been killed by the Nazis, that my father had remarried, and that I was the only blood relative who still remained alive. To my astonishment, I didn't hear from Jean or her parents again for a long time.

However, I did not give up my plans to go to the United States. I told my father, "I have an idea, and it should work out. I will never make the same mistake that I made when I had a chance to save my brother Leiser from the big ghetto.

"Let's go to the HIAS office and tell them that I have relatives in America and see if I can go first. Then I'll bring you over later on."

Sure enough, I went with my father to the HIAS Munich office and told them that I had relatives in America. They asked me where I came from, and I told them I was originally from Latvia. They said that the Latvian quota list was very long, and it would take a long time to obtain visas if we wanted to go together. We hadn't told the HIAS office that we were related, and I said that I wanted to go by myself. I was told that there would be no problems. I was the right age, young enough to be acceptable for immigration, yet old enough to take care of myself. I knew that it would be only a short time before I could send for my father, and I made up my mind that I had to leave.

When I filled out the application, I stated that I was an orphan and had no relatives living in Europe.

Within two months, I was called into the American Consulate in Munich and told that my papers had been accepted. I felt very guilty about leaving my father behind, although I knew it was the best choice. My father was waiting for me in the lobby, and I referred to the statement that I was an orphan, saying, "I buried you."

He answered, "Very good." He was happy that I had this opportunity, and knew that I would send for him as soon as possible.

Although I was still in engineering school, I decided to leave, planning to continue my education in the United States. In fact, I was later accepted by City College of New York (now part of CUNY) and even took the entrance exam in Cooper Union, but I had to earn a living and worked in my profession as a radio and television repairman.

I had kept my cousin's letter and wrote her that I planned to come to America alone; Jean answered that her family was happy with my decision. When I arrived in New York on November 10, 1947, Jean came to pick me up and took me to her house on Van Sicklen Avenue in Brooklyn. I lived in their home until I was able to bring my father and his wife to join me.

I had some difficulty with my luggage when I arrived because I had a tremendous container of Rosenthal china, which my father's friend had asked me to deliver to his relatives in Allentown, Pennsylvania. The Customs Office would not release the package until the people came from Allentown and said that I was their relative who had brought the dishes as part of my marriage preparations. Finally they paid a tariff and received the package.

I arrived in the United States on November 10, 1947, and my father and his wife came on May 29, 1949. I had been in America less than two years, arriving with seven dollars in my pocket, yet I was able to pick them up from the Manhattan pier in my own car. My father had a job as a tailor waiting for him. I had prepared an apartment for them, which we lived in together until my marriage on June 4, 1950. I had kept my promise to bring them to America to a better life.

When I speak in schools, I emphasize to the children that they should remain in school and get an education. An education will help them to a better life in the future. I know because I educated myself. I made sure that I had a trade that I could use in any country in the world, wherever I settled. Without an education, I would have been at the mercy of others, living on charity, so I stress the importance of education.

The principal told the students, "Please look at Mr. Ratz. He is a survivor of the Holocaust. In twenty years there will be no survivors left, only books about them. But you will be able to tell your children that you have seen a live survivor."

The day I arrived in New York, November 10, 1947, my cousin Jean took me to her house and gave me a small room. She was married to Jerry Altholtz, and they had a son, Morty, and a daughter, Hilda. My Uncle Nathan Zahl, Jean's father, also lived with them.

I spent one week at their home, and the second week I took a job at Bressner's Appliance Store, working as a radio mechanic. I had finished one year of college in Germany and had my transcript, but my English wasn't good. Even though I had a job, I planned to continue my education. I registered at Thomas Jefferson High School for night classes in English, and graduated only six months later. Forty years later, I myself taught night school classes in electrnics, radio and television.

My cousin Nat told me to apply at Cooper Union to study engineering. I was included in a group of about 500 people, mostly G.I.s, who had come to take the entrance exam. I passed the first exam, which covered physics, chemistry, and math, but two weeks later I was called back to take an exam in English grammar, literature, and spelling. I wrote that I was handicapped by the language barrier, and failed the exam.

The following year, I received an application to try again, but I felt that I was making good money and didn't have time to attend classes. I decided to take a correspondence course instead. I finished half of the correspondence course, then went to City College of New York. I later dropped out because I couldn't keep up my grades and work at the same time. I was already married and had to support my family, so I left school to work full-time at my television repair business, but I am always learning and ready to experience new things.

12

MARRIAGE AND FAMILY

THE DAY MY FATHER AND HIS WIFE arrived in America, May 29, 1949, I proudly picked them up with my own car. People and friends came over to visit with him, and after a few weeks, my father found an old girl friend whom he had known in "the old country," Chyena Kaplowitz. After they reminisced about old times she told him that she had become a grandmother; her daughter had delivered twins. They were organizing the *Pidyon HaBen* (Redemption of the Firstborn Son), and she invited my father with his wife and son.

I drove to the *Pidyon HaBen*, and as soon as Mrs. Kaplowitz's daughter Dora saw me, she said, "I have a very nice girl for you."

I excitedly asked, "Who is the girl?" and Dora told me that her friend Evelyn worked with the girl. I agreed to arrange a date with her.

It was around Succoth that I met my Doris for the first time, and we walked and talked for hours. After I took her home and made plans for another date, I went home and told my father that I would be dating Doris.

He said, "What's your hurry? I just spoke to our neighbor, and he has a girl for you, too. Her father has five or ten liquor stores, and you wouldn't have to work for the rest of your life."

I replied, "Listen, Papa, Doris is the girl I want to marry."

We had several more dates, and then Doris told me her mother was making a Thanksgiving dinner and planned to invite my father and his wife—and me, naturally.

When we arrived at their home in Brooklyn, it seemed as if everyone in her family was there. Her Uncle Sam kept saying, "*Nu*, official! *Nu*, official!" I was very naive and asked, "What official?" But somehow it became "official."

With my fiancée, Doris—it's official!

About a month later, my bride invited me for supper and after eating, I gave her a "tip"—an engagement ring. And now it was really official.

Our wedding, June 4, 1950, with my father and his wife

My mother-in-law was in charge of preparations for the wedding, which took place on June 4, 1950. Two months before the wedding, we rented an apartment at 1675 Sterling Place in Brooklyn. We honeymooned in Canada, stopping off at Doris's grandmother's farm near Ellenville, New York, on the way back to our own apartment.

Two years later we bought our first home on Beverly Road in Brooklyn.

As a young father my ambition was to guide my children for the future, that in their lives they should help humanity. My children chose fields in health and science to help humanity achieve happier, healthier, longer lives. Compare this to Hitler's henchmen and his collaborators whose aim was to shorten people's lives and to kill as many human beings as possible. My daughter Judy chose health and science to help people have longer lives in the hospital. My son Tevey is a pharmacist, and my son Jeffrey is a doctor of chiropractic. I have Holocaust survivor friends who also persuaded their children to work for humanity in the medical field. They are doctors of cardiology, ophthalmology, gynecology, dentistry, and surgery. I am sure that other Holocaust survivors of the crematoria, the concentration camps, and the death camps who were liberated and settled all over the world, have convinced their children in the same way, to help human beings and not to destroy or kill.

Tevey was born of September 26, 1951, when we lived on Sterling Place in a beautiful apartment. When he was one month old, we made him a *Pidyon HaBen* (Redemption of the Firstborn), and my wife's grandmother roasted ducks for the occasion. A few years later we bought a house on Beverly Road near Kings Highway in Brooklyn.

Our daughter Judy was born on December 2, 1953. She was due in March 1954, but was ten weeks premature. She weighed only two pounds three ounces, and we spent the next ten weeks in the hospital with her. When we finally took her home, she was a beautiful blond baby weighing five pounds, and was smaller than the doll we bought for her.

As time went on, our third child was born on July 9, 1958. When I took Doris to the hospital, she realized that she had forgotten her bathrobe. I rushed back home to pick it up, and as I came in, the phone rang with the news that I already had a beautiful new son. Every person has his own luck in life, even the way he is born.

We feel we are very lucky. We have healthy children; even so it took plenty out of us to raise them, but that is the normal way of life. There is an expression, "little children, little problems; big children, big problems." But I have a different expression, "Little children don't let you sleep and big children don't let you live."

Our son Tevey attended Crown Heights Yeshiva, Yeshiva University High School for Boys, and Brooklyn College. He then studied at Long Island College of Pharmacy where he attained the degree of bachelor of science. On June 30, 1974, he married Toby Stolov, a graduate of Baruch College with a master's degree in education who works in the public school system as an educational evaluator. They have two children, a son, Tracy, who attends Buffalo University, majoring in computer science, and a daughter, Erin, who attends Yeshiva of Flatbush High School.

Tevey and his family, Toby, Tracy and Erin. My wife and I are in front.

Judy attended Crown Heights Yeshiva, Yeshiva University High School for Girls, and Brooklyn College. She studied at Bar Ilan University in Ramat Gan, Israel, where she earned her bachelor of science degree in biology. She then attended Boston Medical School and was awarded a master's degree in microbiology, later achieving a master's degree in epidemiology from New York Medical School. She now works at Jamaica General Hospital as the director of infectious diseases. She married Sidney Fine on November 10, 1985, deliberately choosing the anniversary of the date on which I arrived in America. At the wedding she made a speech and said, "My father came here all by himself with a dream, and today his dream was accomplished. We planned our wedding to coincide with the anniversary of his arrival in America."

Her husband Sidney is a chemist, working for a pharmaceutical company. They have four children, two girls and two boys. The eldest is Sara, next is Elena, third is Aaron David, and fourth is Bryan. They attend yeshiva schools, except for the youngest, two years old at the time of this writing.

Daughter Judy, her husband Sidney and their four children, with me and my wife.

Jeffrey attended Crown Heights Yeshiva and Yeshiva University High School for Boys. He was featured in *Who's Who in High Schools in the United States*. He was graduated from Baruch College and the Cleveland Chiropractic School and is now a successful chiropractor with his own office. He married Pearl Goldberg on July 27, 1980. Pearl helps out in the office and also manages another doctor's office. Pearl and Jeff have four children. Matthew, the oldest, is entering Yeshiva High School; Tara and Avery both attend yeshiva grammar school, and their youngest, David, is still at home at this time.

Dr. Jeffrey Ratz, wife Pearl and their four children. My wife and I are in front.

When my children help people, I feel that that is my revenge on Hitler, who tried to destroy humanity. I demanded of my children that they attain higher education because it has always been my contention that the more educated a person is, the easier his life will be. I have always felt that a good education is necessary in order to provide for the future. I stressed this message continually to my children, and I believe the results bear me out.

I arrived in the United States on November 10, 1947, and two weeks later found a job in Bressner's, a radio-television store. I worked at Bressner's until March 1948, when I got a job installing TV antennas and installing picture tubes into cabinets. In addition, I worked at another firm on Montague Street, installing and repairing projection screen TVs.

In 1949, I took a job as a TV repairman at Bedford Imperial, where I worked until 1952, when I opened my own business, which I operated until 1979. I realized that with the new, lower-priced TVs, the customers would rather buy a new set than repair the old one. I looked around for something else to do, and finally, at the age of fifty-four, decided to apply to the Transit Authority for a job.

Always ready for a challenge, I took the test. Although I was worried about my English skills, I passed the exam and was hired as an electrical technician.

I always got along well with all the other workers, no matter what ethnic group they belonged to. My motto was always, "What can I do for you today?" and my coworkers appreciated my attitude. I walked the tracks, making repairs, and always tried to help out my friends—and I was a friend to everyone.

After two years on the job, I discovered that I needed heart surgery. Again, God was watching over me! I was entitled to full health benefits, having worked two years. If the surgery had been required earlier, I would not have had full health coverage and disability. Once again, I was miraculously in the right place at the right time, and thank God, I came out of surgery and made a full recovery.

The Transit Authority treated me very nicely; my supervisor took me off the line after the operation and gave me an office job. My former foreman laughed and said, "Now you are my boss!"

When I retired in 1990, my fellow employees threw a retirement party for me and gave me a plaque.

13

TRIPS TO MY BIRTHPLACE

WHEN I USED TO TAKE MY MOTHER-IN-LAW, my wife, and her aunt to the United Hebrew Cemetery in Staten Island twice a year where I said the prayers for them, they always used to cry for their fathers, mothers, brothers and uncles.

One day I started to cry. My mother-in-law asked me why I was crying, and I said, "You have a place to go to pray twice a year for your relatives. Where can I go?" My mother and brother were killed in Riga on December 8, 1941, and my father died in Israel on December 8, 1982.

That same day I made up my mind to take a trip, which would include both Riga and Holon, Israel, on the same journey. And I did it in November 1988. Here is my story.

My wife and I had a most exciting experience. After forty-four years, I returned to my birthplace, the city of Riga, on November 20, 1988. I met my cousin, whom I hadn't seen since our liberation from concentration camp in 1945. The city is still very beautiful, but my memories are very sad. The house that I lived in is still standing; the school that I attended, Torah v'Derech Eretz, which during the war was used as the Judenrat building in the large ghetto, is now a Russian school. The day we were there the Russian children took a walk during their recess period. (Latvia was still under Soviet control in 1988.)

Torah v'Derech Eretz School which I attended, later used as the Judenrat building in the big ghetto

The same day I visited the forest of Rumbuli where approximately 30,000 women, old men, and children were slaughtered and buried in mass graves. The Russian government would not allow the mention of the word "Jew" on any memorial, but a plaque in several languages, including Yiddish, states, "Here lie the victims of Fascism."

There was a new feeling of glasnost abroad, and people were free to come and go to Rumbuli after forty-six years. My wife and I were among the first Jews to come from America to visit Rumbuli. I took pictures of all the graves and said Kaddish and

Memorial stone at Rumbuli Forest

Kel Moleh Rachamim at the gravesides. Afterward, we visited the Riga ghetto, which is still inhabited but at this time by non-Jews. The synagogue that was once in that area is now an apartment building. The only shul still in existence, the Petau Synagogue, is in the center of the city, which saved it from being burned. I went to daven there every day and on Shabbat we had two *hazonim* (cantors). Unfortunately there are almost no religious people left, and the assimilation is very sad to witness. The Rabbi Emeritus learned Talmud with us every morning before davening. Almost everyone in the shul says Kaddish. The old rabbi is a *mohel* and a *shochet* (ritual slaughterer), but now he is very frail, so they have a new rabbi, about forty years of age, educated in Hungary. They bake matzoth for Passover in the lower part of the shul, sending shipments of them to the big cities in Russia. Twice yearly a *shochet* comes to slaughter, so they have kosher meat and salami and other by-products for Rosh Hashanah and Passover.

There is a new awareness of religion and Jewish culture in Riga. We were told that they plan to have four classes in Hebrew and Yiddish in the shul, and I was asked if I could see to it that they would receive Hebrew and Yiddish books. Lectures are held every month in the old Jewish Theater, and many young people are involved in this project.

While we were there, a delegation of Jews came from France to memorialize the victims of Rumbuli. They had been to the Forest of Babi Yar, and after visiting Rumbuli they planned to go the Pannar Forest near Vilna.

Our first trip to Riga

NOVEMBER 19, 1988, 9 P.M.
THE NIGHT BEFORE DEPARTURE FROM NEW YORK
We packed four full suitcases, two for Riga, one for Jerusalem, and one for ourselves. We filled the suitcases for Riga and Jerusalem with presents and the other with food and clothing. In the middle of the night it started to rain, and rained all night and the next day.

NOVEMBER 20, 1988, 8 A.M.
I went to shul to pray as usual, and at 8:45 after the services, everyone gave money to me to distribute as charity to poor people and yeshivot in Israel. Our purpose is threefold in Riga: to do some groundwork for a monument to the victims of the Holocaust, from us in the United States in conjunction with survivors in Riga, to go to the site where my mother and brothers

were murdered and buried; and to see my cousin, Mottel, whom I hadn't seen in over forty-three years and his wife, Ida. It was also the forty-seventh year of mourning and memorial service for my family in the Hebrew calendar, which came out on November 27 in 1988; it was the eighteenthth day of Kislev, which was December 8, 1941.

There were two reasons for our trip to Israel: to see my step-mother; and to visit my father's grave on the anniversary of his death, which in 1988 came out on December 1, the twenty-second day of Kislev. In the year of his death, 1982, the twenty-seond of Kislev came out on December 8, which was the day we would return home from our trip in 1988. This was the first time that I would be able to visit the graves of both of my parents on the anniversaries of their death, and I was very emotional.

From 10 A.M. until 2 P.M., good wishes from our friends and neighbors kept coming in by phone, invoking a wonderful trip for us.

3 P.M.

We left the house to begin our journey. Our first stop before the flight was at Jeffrey's house where our family had gathered so that we could say goodbye to all our children and grandchildren. We celebrated my wife's forthcoming birthday with a surprise cake. We said goodbye, kissed everybody, and finally, at 6 P.M., we left for the airport.

It had begun to rain the night before, and rain continued to pour down. It was very foggy, and I hoped we would be able to leave on time. The flight was scheduled for 9 P.M.; we arrived for the 6:30 check-in and decided to check one suitcase for Frankfurt, our stopover. Since we would be returning to Frankfurt in one week, we didn't need to drag this suitcase, destined for Jerusalem, all over Russia. The PanAm agent told us we would have enough time to put this suitcase into a locker in Frankfurt for the week and to pick it up on the way to Israel the following week.

We boarded the plane not at 8 P.M. as scheduled, but at 9 P.M. we were still waiting on the tarmac, and the plane finally took off at 10:15. The delay was caused by the terrible fog, and we lost about two hours. We arrived in Frankfurt just in time to board our Moscow flight, and didn't have time to store the suitcase as planned. We left the luggage stub with the PanAm personnel and asked them to put the bag in storage until our return.

We left Frankfurt on time on PanAm Flight 914 and arrived in Moscow at 6 P.M. on November 21 as scheduled. Our next flight was at 9:30 P.M., which gave us enough time to board our Riga plane. We were taken to a small booth to have our passports stamped. The inspector was a very young man who began to speak to us in Russian. I didn't answer in that language, so he finally switched to English. He stamped our visas, and at last we were ready for our suitcases.

It took some time before I could get a handcart for our luggage, and then it was just a matter of waiting for our baggage arrived from the PanAm flight. We waited from 6:20 P.M. until 10 P.M., at which point we had already missed our connection to Riga. Intourist put us, with the other people who had missed their flights, onto a bus that took us to a hotel, the Aeroflot.

We had to go through Customs again, and once more the inspector spoke to us in Russian. I refused to speak to him in Russian, and he finally spoke in English. He ordered me to open the zipper of my hand luggage, and found my Tallit and Tefillin. He questioned me about them, but at last he let us go.

We dragged and carried our three suitcases and hand luggage to the bus. The bus was at least twenty-five years old and cold. Next to me on the bus was a woman from Ethiopia. She was so cold she sat bundled up to the eyes with her hands covering her ears, while I sat with my coat open. I was reminded of the time when I worked for the German army in 1941, and saw the volunteer soldiers from Spain who were unable to take the cold. We arrived at the hotel at 12:15 A.M. where we were given a cold, dirty room. It was 12:47 A.M. on November 22, 1988. We had to rise at 5 A.M. to be ready for the next flight to Riga at the National Airport.

At 6:15 A.M. someone knocked at the door, telling us to get ready. We had been ready all night! At 8:00 A.M. we were at the airport to check in our suitcases, and at 9:55 we were scheduled for takeoff. Moscow has two airports, the International where we had arrived from Frankfurt, and the National, which is for Aeroflot flights only. By the way, the Soviet Union was fifty or sixty years behind the times in everything. When we arrived at the National Airport, we found people had been sleeping on benches and on the floor overnight. The place was a mess. Finally at 9:30 A.M. on November 22 we were told to board the plane, and at 9:55 on the dot we took off from Moscow for Riga, in a plane filled to standing room with soldiers.

I was very excited to be on the verge of seeing my cousin again. We had been in touch by letter for many years, except for one long break in the mid-70s when I suddenly lost contact with my cousin. We had been writing letters to each other steadily, and then the letters stopped without explanation. Many years later, I found out what had happened.

My cousin was an important man in Russia. After his miraculous return from the front, when the war ended he was accepted by the prestigious university in Riga and later was one of the scientists who worked on the Sputnik program. Mottel (Max) was well thought of by the Communist Party, but during the '70s the Communists decided that my cousin should become a spy and report any anti-Communist conversations that he heard.

He was ordered to wear a hidden microphone and listen to conversations in the shuls and public places. The truth was that people did meet in shuls to discuss world affairs and communist reactions, and if there was disloyalty, that would be the place to find out about it. Mottel didn't want to become a spy, and told the communists that he never went anywhere. He said, "I don't have a wife, I don't have a family. I don't have family anywhere in the world. I don't go to the synagogue. I don't go anywhere. I wouldn't be a good choice to spy on the people."

In order to prove that he had no contact with anyone, he stopped going out of his apartment except to work and for the basic necessities, and he stopped writing to me so that he wouldn't be accused of being in league with someone in America.

For a long time I was afraid that Mottel had died. I was very happy when, after a four- or five-year silence, he again began writing to me. Apparently, he was no longer considered useful as a spy and was permitted to carry on a normal life. Our correspondence resumed and continues even now.

We finally arrived in Riga on the third day, November 22, a Tuesday, at 12:55 P.M. At 1:10 P.M. our cousin Ida saw us for the first time in our lives, but we didn't see my cousin Max. They had come to the airport the previous night, and he had become so nervous that he thought he was having a heart attack. He decided to wait for us at home, where the atmosphere was less tense. We had tried to call or send a telegram to let them know we had been delayed, but to no avail; there was no way to get in touch with individuals. Ida called him from the airport to let him know that we had finally arrived and were going to the hotel.

We had a limousine and guide waiting for us. Our luggage was loaded into the car, and we all got in. We drove through Riga, which was referred to as Little Paris, and is still the cultural center of the Baltic States. The Hotel Latvia is located in the middle of the city and is very tall for a city like Riga. Finnish workers were hired to build the hotel because the Russian laborers didn't produce, but the Finns were sent away before the hotel was completed, and the Russians finished the job.

Riga had no liquor stores, but since perestroika every bottle of vodka was rationed. One had to stand in line for hours to get one bottle, but the people managed to find a way to make their own.

We finally arrived at the Hotel Latvia, and at 2:05 P.M., for the first time in nearly forty-four years, my cousin and I met face to face. We hugged each other silently for a few minutes and then we cried like babies. It was like a miracle and a dream come true for both of us. We gazed at each other, amazed that we were finally together. It didn't seem possible after forty-four years of separation.

The hotel was packed with people from all over the communist world. The automatic elevators worked, but one was lucky to get on, it was so crowded. Our room was very nice. The bathroom had a unique heating system: A towel rack was mounted on the wall with a heating element in it. It served not only to warm the room but also to dry the wet towels.

The room had no television, but a radio that had a volume control and an on-off switch. It carried only one government-controlled station that was on the air only at certain hours and played American pop music from the 1930s. As I say, the Russians are fifty or sixty years behind everyone else.

My cousin promised that he would stay with us for the next five days; we would be inseparable. We stayed in the hotel for a few hours and then left for Mottel's apartment.

We spent the rest of the afternoon and night with my cousins. Ida and Mottel have a very nice two-room apartment. One room serves as the kitchen and bedroom and the other is the living, dining, and extra bedroom. They were so happy for us to be there, and we were very excited too. Ida made a dinner of gefilte fish, teiglach, cookies, and coffee with all kinds of liqueurs. Mottel even made sure that all the dishes and pots were new, kosher, and got a kilo of kosher salami from the shul.

8 P.M., NOVEMBER 22

My cousin went down to the street to find a taxi, which took us back to the hotel. I was so excited that I couldn't sleep all night.

I got up at 7 A.M. on November 23, dressed, and said my prayers in the hotel room. We ate breakfast and then were ready for the trip that I had dreamed of for the past forty-seven years and planned for the last ten. Now my dream was coming true. I feel that I am a very lucky man.

10 A.M., NOVEMBER 23

I was ready, waiting for Max and his cousin to take my wife and me all over the city of Riga for three or four hours. I had very mixed feelings seeing this beautiful city, which holds very bad memories for me.

We traveled throughout Riga, visiting our past. Our first stop was the infamous Rumbuli Forest. I tried to shake away my thoughts, but they kept returning to what happened on December 8, 1941, to my family. I took many pictures of every grave. There are six graves for adults and one for children. My cousin was my guide and told me that this was the first time that I could go to Rumbuli Forest as a free man, without disturbance. We prayed and said Kaddish and *Kel Moleh Rachamim*. We found a stone marked in Latvian and a monument inscribed in Russian and Yiddish, just a little stone imprinted with the characters 30 xi 1941, and 8 xii 1941. It was a very, very emotional experience. We hugged one another and cried like babies.

After Rumbuli, we drove into the ghetto. Max showed me the house at 37 Ludzasiela Street where we had lived in the large

Memorial stone at Rumbuli, engraved with the dates 30 November 1941 and 8 December 1941

ghetto for about two months before the Nazis closed it and drove out my mother and brothers to be murdered. Then he took me to the house in the small ghetto where my father, he, and I had lived with seven other men. It was from that house that we were taken to Lenta and then to KZ Stutthof in Germany.

We drove to the old neighborhood where we had lived before the war and saw our old homes and the yeshiva school I had attended. We had lived at No. 6 Basnitzasiela until my Bar Mitzvah and then at No. 80 Moscowasiela until the war broke out and we moved to the large ghetto. The synagogue that we had attended had been turned into an apartment house. The other Riga synagogue is now an empty lot.

I was amazed to find that all the houses in which we had lived in Riga and even in the ghetto were still standing, while lots next to them and across the street had been destroyed.

1 P.M., NOVEMBER 23

We arrived back at the hotel, and again Max and I started to talk about our past life. At 2:30 we took a city bus back to my cousin's house where we chatted until 5:15. We agreed to meet at a lecture given by Professor Meyer Westerman who had lived through the ghetto and camps and lectured about the Holocaust years, 1941–1945. It was very interesting to see about 350–400 young people at the lecture. After his speech, he discussed the erection of monument in memory of the murdered Jews who were killed in Rumbuli.

I took the opportunity to go up to the podium and introduced myself to Professor Westerman. I told him that I had come from the United States the previous day and my mission was to help put up the monument in conjunction with the Riga Jews who had survived the war and who lived in America, England, Israel, South Africa, and Australia. I made an appointment for the next day with Mrs. Rapina, one of the heads of the Culture Committee, who was in charge of the money for the monument.

As we returned to the hotel, two people stopped us, and we discussed our trip with them. At 8:45 we walked into our hotel room, ready to go to sleep after our hectic and emotionally draining day. We were exhausted from our trip through Rumbuli, the ghetto, and the city itself, to say nothing of our long journey from New York.

I couldn't sleep and at 2 A.M. on November 24, I got out of bed. All the previous day, from 10 A.M. until 1 P.M., with my cousin as our guide, with his cousin as our driver, my wife and I had visited the sites of the greatest tragedies of my life. I sit in

With my cousin in front of the house in the ghetto, No. 37 Ludzasiela

the hotel bathroom, writing and crying, thinking of the pictures I had taken of Rumbuli, of the graves and the monuments, of the homes where I had spent my young life with my parents and brothers, of the school I had attended so happily. The house at No. 2 Puskiniela where my grandfather had been a shoemaker and where my older brother and I had had our Bar Mitzvahs and from which we had seen the destruction of the Latvian and Rigan Jews.

At 5 A.M. on November 24, I wrote this message for my children.

Children:
   Your mother is sleeping. I am writing these words for you, and I am crying.

I can't sleep, seeing the house at 37 Ludzasiela, where we had lived in the large ghetto. I am crying, thinking of the night the ss chased all the men out into the street in the middle of the night, and how they killed all the Jewish policemen in the small ghetto. I remember being sent out of the small ghetto to Lenta, where I was reunited with my father before we were sent to kz Stutthof and Salaspils Death Camp.

On November 30, 1941, the Germans initiated the first Aktion. They took the people out, emptying the ghetto up to Daugavpilsiela, and one week later, on December 7–8, they cleared the rest of the ghetto.

Finally the long night was over, and on the morning of November 24, I received a phone call from a Mr. Gart. He thanked me for my information about the Riga Jews memorial that I had given at the lecture, and gave me tips about where to go to see Riga's remaining Jews.

11 A.M.

My cousin and his wife came to the hotel and were at our service for our next venture. Doris and Ida decided to go shopping while Max and I went to see Mrs. Rapina.

I took pictures of the buildings in Old Riga and the building where my Jewish teacher had lived. Then we went to the office building where the Culture Committee maintains its headquarters and took the old-fashioned elevator up to Room 427A. A charming lady who spoke six or seven languages fluently sat at a desk answering the incessantly ringing phone. She had been expecting my arrival, and we talked for an hour. The book about the survivors of Riga, *Muted Voices*, will be placed in the Cultural Committee museum and will be translated into Russian. Mrs. Rapina gave me a letter of thanks to bring to my community in New York, and we agreed to maintain steady contact.

I had fulfilled my obligations, and thought, as we always like to feel, "mission undertaken, mission accomplished."

2:15 P.M.

Doris and Ida had gone shopping and bought two samovars. Max and I took trolley car no. 6 in the middle of the city and went sightseeing on our way to my cousin's house at no. 1A Yuglasiela where our wives were waiting.

On our sightseeing expedition I took more pictures, including the exterior and interior of the Petau Shul. A woman opened the door for us after we promised to return to daven mincha and ma'ariv, which we did. At 4:15 we took a taxi to the shul, where eight men waited for us. Then the rabbi came, and

Inside the Petau Shul, the only synagogue remaining in Riga

including us, there were now eleven men, more than enough for a minyan. We spoke to the men, and I took more pictures.

We returned to the hotel at 6:15 and waited for Doris and Ida. We talked about our past, present, and future from 7 P.M. until after nine, when my cousins left, and Doris and I went to sleep.

FRIDAY, NOVEMBER 25, 10 A.M.
It seemed like a nice day. The sun was out, and it wasn't cold. Max and Ida arrived at 12:15 to celebrate Doris's birthday with flowers. I surprised Doris with a birthday card I had brought from home. We prepared for Shabbat, and my cousin and I planned to go to shul together.

At 4:15 my cousin and I left for shul. We were surprised to meet people from Paris and Lyons, France. One man introduced himself as Dr. Marc Aron, the president of B'nai B'rith of France, personal physician to Premier Mitterand. Another man was Maurice Nouschi, a journalist from Paris who had come to Rumbuli on a special mission for the Sunday *Haskara* (Memorial Service). The group from France consisted of about twenty-five people, doctors and journalists with their wives. They really touched me with their concern and their interest in the victims of Riga and their survivors.

In shul we heard a nice *hazan* (cantor), Moshe Ahron, whose singing was excellent. It was a pity to see 650 empty seats in a building that can accommodate 700.

We returned to the hotel room, where I made Kiddush on wine we had brought with us and cried again. We dined on gefilte fish that Doris had brought from America, my cousin's salami, turkey roll, and crackers. Ida couldn't believe her eyes when she saw our disposable plastic dishes and utensils; she had never seen such things. We talked until Max and Ida went home. To us it was a miracle impossible to describe.

After supper we walked down into the lobby and found the French people whom we had met at the shul; they were also staying at the same hotel. We spoke again about Rumbuli Forest. I had gone to the forest on Wednesday, and they planned to go on the following Sunday for the *Haskara*. We talked for an hour, and then Doris and I went back upstairs to rest. My nightmares kept me from sleeping for the rest of the night. I tossed and turned until about seven in the morning, then dressed for shul. It was still dark; at that time of year, sunrise in Riga is about 9:30 A.M.

I went down to the lobby to wait for Max to walk me to shul. He came about 8 A.M. and we left for the Petau Shul, where we found three old people who learned Talmud until services started around 9:30 A.M.

That Shabbat we had two *hazonim*, Samuel Nachamowitz and Moshe Ahron, who were both excellent. The congregation con-

The French delegation at the Hotel Latvia

sisted of fifty people, including the contingent from France, plus Doris and Ida. I was called up to the lectern during the Torah reading and *bentched gomel* (recited a special prayer of thanksgiving for surviving danger). The *gabbai* (sexton) recited *Kel Moleh Rachamim* for my family, who had perished in the war. It broke my heart. The *gabbai* repeated the prayer for my cousin's family and for the families of those in the shul who held Yahrzeit (anniversary) for their families who were killed in Rumbuli Forest.

During the reading of the Torah portion, a man came over to me and said he was a refusenik—that is, someone who had applied to the Soviet government to emigrate and had been refused. We discussed getting a supply of Hebrew books for the Jews in Riga so that they could learn Hebrew prior to going to Israel. He accompanied us back to the hotel, and I continued to speak to him about the books. I had strong hopes that I would be able to help him with this important project.

When we returned to our room, Doris had our lunch ready. I made Kiddush, and we ate and talked and talked some more. An hour later, we again prepared to go to shul for Mincha, after which we had *Seuda Shlishis* (the third Shabbat meal), which consisted of vodka, fish, crackers, and herring. We went to shul for Ma'ariv, after which our Yahrzeit started.

It was the first time in my life that I was with my cousin and friends to commemorate our Yahrzeit together. After Ma'ariv I had an appointment with the French delegation of Jews to speak to them as a survivor of Rumbuli. Later I met another refusenik, eighty-two-year-old Samuel Abramsohn, who speaks French, German, Russian, Yiddish, Hebrew, Latvian and English. He too spoke to the French delegation, telling them about the French Jews who were killed in Riga. He worked with me to raise money for the monument. It was a very emotional and interesting experience.

I was interviewed by Dr. Marc Aron of the French B'nai B'rith and Maurice Nouschi, who is a member of the Association Souvenir de Rumbuli. Although I spoke English, Hebrew, German, and Yiddish, some of the delegates spoke only French. My words were translated into French while the observers constantly watched my face. Doris had already gone up to the room to rest, and after an hour or so, I followed her. I made a phone call to a friend with whom I hadn't spoken for fifty-one years. He was shocked and happy to hear from me.

The next morning, November 27, I waited for Max to accompany me to shul. On the way to shul we once again cried like babies when we realized that we had only about four hours together before Doris and I were to leave. We arrived at the Petau Shul for morning services and said Kaddish together once more before leaving the shul. I was filled with sorrow, not knowing when I would return, not knowing if we would see each other again.

My cousin stayed with us until noon when the limousine arrived with our escort to the airport. Our drive to the airport led past Lenta labor camp, where I had spent a year and a half until I was taken to Salaspils and then back to Lenta for three more weeks before being transported to Stutthof. I recognized the watchtower as we passed.

We arrived at the airport at 12:45 P.M. on November 27, and at 1:25 the plane took off for Moscow, where we arrived at 2:55. It is hard to describe saying goodbye to my cousin. We held each other and hugged for a few minutes without saying a word, but our thoughts—our thoughts communicated everything. For the last time we cried together and finally kissed each other goodbye.

At the airport, a bus took us part of the way onto the field, and then we walked to the plane and up the steps. It was cold in the plane and the passengers' faces were cold, no smiles visible. As before, the plane was packed with people. Within minutes we were airborne. We were not served any food, but the flight attendants sold tacky souvenirs.

We arrived at the National Airport in Moscow and had to transfer to our connecting flight at the International Airport. The Intourist representative put us on a bus to take us to the International. While we waited to go through Customs, Doris went shopping. She found a store that sold souvenirs; although the prices were marked in Russian rubles, the clerks accepted only American dollars.

Finally we went to the Customs Office with our papers and luggage, but we didn't know that we needed one more document to leave Moscow. The office was so chaotic that it took half an hour to find the document in English. At last we filled out all the documents and had them stamped. We waited for our Lufthansa flight to Frankfurt, which seemed to start on time, but returned from the runway with a flat tire. It took three hours to replace that flat tire at Moscow's International Airport so our flight was delayed for that period.

After the plane finally took off, the stewards told us that they did not have kosher food for us. We had had no kosher food on the PanAm flight from New York to Frankfurt, and we had the same luck now: no kosher food from Moscow to Frankfurt.

Because of the delay, we now had to spend the night of November 28 in Frankfurt, and after our arrival we began to search for the Hotel Sheridan. We walked for half an hour and finally found it. There was a long line for hotel rooms, but due to a number of cancellations, we managed to get a room. It was 1:30 in the morning, and the price of the room was 360 marks ($750), which allowed us to use the room until 6:30 A.M. We paid 72 marks (about $150) per hour to spend five hours in the hotel!

The next morning we went to the airport to find the luggage that had been left for us one week earlier. I went from one PanAm employee to the other, and back and forth to the Customs agent, for over two hours until I found out that the luggage was going back to New York. We were in luck this time; the airport was fogged in, and no planes could land or depart. We hoped they would find our suitcase in Frankfurt, and we would receive it in Tel Aviv.

Our flight to Tel Aviv was delayed because of the fog, so we all sat in a small room, watched over by guards. We underwent a body search, and our luggage was examined as well, but we finally left two hours late. While we were waiting, I called PanAm again and spoke to yet another agent about our suitcase. The woman said she knew nothing about it, and again I started my story from the beginning.

Finally we arrived in Tel Aviv; our first stop there was the Customs Office. We got our own suitcase, but the bag with the gifts did not arrive so we made a report to the Lost and Found office. We took a taxi to visit my stepmother in Bat Yam; she was surprised that we were three hours late, but on this trip three hours late was nothing!

As soon as I unpacked, I made some phone calls, because people were waiting for me. Doris and I finally went to bed around 11 P.M. I awoke at 7 A.M. on November 29, bathed, dressed, prayed, and prepared to travel again. Until yesterday we had traveled by plane, but now we would fly by bus. At 10 A.M. we boarded our bus to Tel Aviv, arriving at 10:30, then the second bus to Jerusalem, arriving at 12 noon and finally bus number three took us to the Kotel, arriving at 12:20. Our fourth bus landed us in the middle of modern Jerusalem, where we had falafel with coffee at an outdoor café, chatting with some Swedish people. They pointed out a Swedish car, a Volvo, which was parked in the wrong place with the wrong license plate; it was taken apart by the Israeli bomb squad.

We took our fifth bus to visit our nephew in Ramot, arriving at 3 P.M., and met the young couple and their children. After taking pictures we boarded our sixth bus to meet some friends from New York in Hotel Larrome, took our seventh bus there, and took more pictures. Then we jumped on yet another bus to the terminal, where we boarded the bus from Jerusalem to Tel Aviv. We arrived at 9:30 P.M. and went back to Bat Yam, finally reaching home at 10 P.M. I had received two phone calls and made return calls to my friends Zipora and Moshe, whom I hoped to see before we left Israel.

NOVEMBER 30

My wife and I went for a walk in Bat Yam by the sea from 11 A.M. to 1 P.M. At 4 P.M. we went to shul for my father's Yahrzeit and took pictures of the Yahrzeit tablets, which had been put up in the shul where my father had davened every day. Every year when I go to Israel for his Yahrzeit I pray at his shul.

When I came back from shul I met Boruch Steinman, a friend whom I hadn't seen for fifty-two years. He told me how and when my brother Mendel had been killed. Until then I had said Kaddish for my mother and brothers on the eighteenth day of Kislev and for my father on the twenty-second of Kislev, but Boruch gave me a new date to say Kaddish for my older brother Mendel. The English date was about June 24, 1942.

Boruch's family was from the small town of Barafka, where my father's family had lived, and he was able to tell me how my father's relatives were killed. Boruch Steinman was the only survivor of his family; his brother, Menachem, was my friend who had been killed during the burning of the Gogol Street Shul on July 4, 1941. Boruch had escaped from the Germans into Russia, had been wounded three times, had returned to Riga and found only graves. He had come to Israel to visit his relatives there. We spoke for an hour, until finally we retired at 11 P.M.

THURSDAY, DECEMBER 1

I arose at 5 A.M. and went to shul to pray. I was called to the Torah and said *Kel Molei Rachamim* and Kaddish. I returned home at 7:45, and after a brief rest prepared for my father' *Haskara*. At 1:45 my nephew took us to Holon Cemetery. We arrived to find our friends waiting for us.

We went to my father's grave, recited *Tehillim* (Psalms) and said Kaddish. My friend recited the *Kel Molei Rachamim* while I cried, and then we left. We found memorial monuments for the Latvian Jews, among others. The inscription on one monument states that bones from Rumbuli Forest are buried there.

We had a busy schedule for Friday, December 2. After our usual morning routine we prepared to travel to Tel Aviv. At 11 A.M. we took the no. 25 bus to the corner of Ben Gurion and Dizengoff where we met our friends Zipora, Moshe, Yosef, and

My father's monument in Holon, Israel

Tusha. We walked to the new mall; Doris, of course, window-shopped in all the beautiful stores. The mall is quite impressive; it reminded us of midtown Manhattan, although it was even more exclusive and very expensive.

We took the bus back to Bat Yam and prepared for Shabbat. Our Friday night meal was rather sad as we realized that after Shabbat we were to return to America. The next day I met a man who had been my father's friend. I spent some time reminiscing with him, and then returned home. After Shabbat we lit the Hanukkah menorah and spoke to friends who had come to visit.

At 9:30 that night, we watched a television program about Riga and the Jewish culture there. The news program featured the story of an Aeroflot plane that had been hijacked from Russia. I hoped our flight would not be delayed because of the hijacking.

Our suitcase full of presents had still not arrived. We hoped to find it in New York or Tel Aviv. At 10 P.M. our taxi arrived, and we headed out for the airport.

DECEMBER 4, 12:30 A.M.

I had the good luck to find our suitcase in the Lost and Found department at Tel Aviv's Ben-Gurion Airport. I phoned my stepmother immediately to tell her that I had found the bag. I took out our few garments from the bag and left it filled with gifts for my stepmother and my nephew's family.

Our flight took off on time with no complications. We had a smooth flight and arrived at 6:10 A.M. Naturally, Doris had bought presents for everyone. My son Jeffrey picked us up and took us to his house where I had left my car. We arrived at our own home at 8 A.M., and I immediately left for shul, arriving in time for the reading of the Torah and to *bentch gomel* again.

Monument in Holon, Israel, to the Latvian martyrs

When I returned home I made a few calls and changed my clothes. Then Doris and I left at 12 noon to celebrate our good friends' fiftieth wedding anniversary. After giving gifts to our children and grandchildren, we finally went home, and planned to be at work the next day.

Sure enough, we got up on December 5 at 5:30 A.M. and started the usual routine, and then it was back to work. Yes, this was some trip, from November 19 until December 5, 1988.

14

OVERCOMING
HEALTH PROBLEMS

WHEN I WAS NINE, I had scarlet fever and was placed in an isolation ward in the hospital, where no visitors were allowed.

The second time I entered the hospital was March 13, 1945,
when I had typhus and I didn't even know how I got to the hospital in Lauenburg, Germany. Again I was on an isolation ward,
but at least this time my father was with me, also suffering from
typhus. This was after our liberation by the Russian army, as
described in a previous chapter. We didn't even know about
each other for several weeks, until the delirium of the fever left
us. I was in the same ward and in the bed next to my father, but
neither of us knew where we were or who else was there.

The third time I went to the hospital I wasn't in isolation, but
still had no visitors, because I had no family. I was in Landsberg, Germany, in the DP camp, and had my tonsils taken out in
July 1947. The DP camp had set aside one building that was
used as a hospital for survivors. Some of the patients were ill,
but there was also a maternity ward, and a boy was born in this
hospital. His name was Israel Jacobowitz, and thirty-five years
later, he was my cardiac surgeon when I had my bypass surgery!

The fourth time I was hospitalized was in Washingtonville, New York, in July 1961, and this time I had visitors. Of course, my lovely wife came to see me with friends from the bungalow colony where we stayed in Monroe, New York. At that time, I had my own business as a television repairman, and I didn't want to take a two-week vacation because I felt I would lose customers if I closed the business for a long period. I decided instead that I would work only four days a week, and take long weekends to be with my wife and children at the bungalow colony. Obviously, I had to work harder to accomplish in four days what I usually did in five.

I also sold and installed air conditioners, and of course the summer was the busy season. At the same time, my father and his wife decided to spend the summer in Israel, and left me in charge of their property, a small apartment building, which needed constant supervision.

Finally, all this stress caught up with me and I suffered from chest pains, alone in the house on a Tuesday night. I was a little worried, and decided to go to the mountains early that week, so I left Wednesday morning. As soon as I arrived, I went to a doctor in Highland Mills, near our bungalow colony. He immediately had me admitted into the hospital. I was lucky to have averted a heart attack. I didn't even realize at the time how good God had been to me. My life had been in danger, and I hadn't even realized it.

In 1981, we went to the World Gathering of Holocaust Survivors in Israel. Doris and I and our friend Zipora were walking in Tel Aviv when I found I couldn't keep up with them, and I had terrible pains in my chest, but the pain passed, and I shrugged it off, and we returned to New York.

When I went to shul for services one Shabbat night, I told my good friend, Rabbi Ben Zion Pittom, about my chest pains, and he introduced me to Dr. Israel Jacobowitz. I told him about my problem, and he gave me his business card as well as a referral to Dr. Marc Sheldon, a cardiologist in New York City.

Dr. Sheldon recommended that I have an angiogram, but I told him that I was too busy. This was in late December, and I was organizing a weekend hotel retreat for the Flatbush Park Jewish Center. I didn't want to take time for medical exams, so Dr. Sheldon told me I could wait until January for the angiogram.

Doris and I left for the hotel retreat on a Thursday, in the middle of a terrible storm. There were practically no cars or trucks on Route 17, the road to the hotel, but I felt I had an obligation to go since I had organized the whole weekend.

People kept arriving at the hotel all day Friday, and I took care of the arrangements for everyone. An astonishing thing happened on Friday night at dinnertime. I was standing at the entrance to the dining room, making sure that everyone was seated properly. Another group was also at the hotel, and suddenly one of the female guests started yelling, "Who is that man?" She was pointing at me, and Doris said that I was her husband.

"But I know that man!" the woman continued to shout. Doris calmed her down, and she asked where I was from originally. When Doris told her that I was from Riga, she shouted, "I know him! He was in Landsberg!"

It turned out that she had been in Landsberg at the time that I was attending the ORT school there. She had married a Mr. Jakubowitz, and a bachelor friend of mine had rented a room from them in Landsberg, where I visited him. We had a surprise reunion, after thirty-four years. Everyone was very excited about it, and it was written up in the hotel newsletter.

We returned home very excited, and I called Dr. Sheldon to make the appointment for the angiogram. He scheduled it for January 11, 1982, a Tuesday morning, at St. Vincent's Hospital, but after I was admitted, I was told that due to an emergency, I had been rescheduled for the next day.

I was very disappointed; I didn't want to waste another whole day in the hospital. I requested that the angiogram be performed early in the morning of the 12th; I said, "Maybe I'm also an emergency." I really just wanted to leave the hospital as soon as possible.

My dinner was brought in at 5 P.M., and I was upset to find that it wasn't a kosher meal. I requested that the tray be exchanged for a kosher food tray, but to no avail. I told the nurse that I was leaving, but I had no clothes and no choice. I had to stay in the hospital. In the morning I put on my Tallit and Tefillin and prayed that the angiogram would be performed safely. It felt very strange to pray under the crucifix that hung on the wall of St. Vincent's, but I knew that God heard my prayers.

At 8 A.M., I was taken for the angiogram. Dr. Sheldon was waiting for me on a different floor. I hadn't realized I was walking around with a time bomb in my chest until I saw the staff change color as they read the angiogram. The test showed that my arteries were almost completely blocked, and they recommended that major surgery be performed the next day.

Dr. Sheldon and his assistant wheeled me into a different room, where I was attached to a monitor and kept in isolation. When Doris arrived, she couldn't find me. I was under the supervision of a special nurse and hooked up to a machine by a whole slew of wires. I later found out that it was a heart/lung machine to prevent a heart attack until I could be operated on the next day.

When the male nurse came in to shave my chest, I tried to joke with him, saying that he shouldn't use a straight razor, just an electric razor, but he didn't even laugh.

I didn't know until after the operation that Dr. Jacobowitz performed a quintuple bypass on me. It was a miracle that I hadn't had a heart attack previously, since so many major arteries were almost completely blocked.

Even before my surgery, I had been taking several types of heart medication, and I told Dr. Sheldon that I wanted to stop taking the pills, which gave me terrible headaches and pains. Dr. Sheldon said I could gradually wean myself from the medication.

When I arrived home after the surgery, I had many visitors. My neighbor asked me if it was a holiday, because so many people were at my house. I told him that it was a holiday for me; it was a miracle that I was alive!

After the operation, I told my doctors that I planned to go to visit my father in Israel. Dr. Sheldon gave me the OK, but Dr. Jacobowitz said I would have to wait several months. We compromised, and I made arrangements to travel to Israel before Passover. I traveled alone, and met a group of people on the plane who called themselves "born-again Christians." I told them, "I was born again for the third time." When they asked for an explanation, I said, "The first time I was born, it was the natural way. I was born the second time when I was liberated from concentration camp, and I recently had a quintuple bypass—that was when I was born again for the third time." I showed them my yarmulke, proof that I am Jewish.

My father was very happy to see me again, even though I had been there just one year before for the World Gathering of Holocaust Survivors. He hadn't known I was sick, and now I got a hero's welcome. I stayed in Israel for two weeks, enjoying the warmth and sunshine. I was taking blood thinners and found the cold in Brooklyn hard to bear. Slowly I weaned myself off the medications, except for nitroglycerin, which I held onto for seven years in case of pain.

I visited Israel twice more in 1982. My father had a stroke in July, and I went to see him then, and on December 8 he passed away. Naturally, I went back for the funeral and to make arrangements for the monument.

Although I occasionally visited Dr. Sheldon for routine checkups, I once met Dr. Jacobowitz in shul. He asked me if I had seen Dr. Sheldon recently, and I said since I felt well, I hadn't. He insisted on coming home from shul with me and examining me. He told me to come to his office in Maimonides Hospital so that he could check me more thoroughly. After the exam, I took out my checkbook, and he said, "Jack, are you crazy? For you there is no charge."

He advised that I see a cardiologist regularly and recommended Dr. Bernard Goldblatt. I said, "Bernie? He's my son's best friend! They had a band together when they were kids!"

I met Dr. Jacobowitz's mother in shul, and we began chatting. She mentioned that her son had been born in Landsberg, Germany, in a DP camp hospital. I asked her when he had been born, and it turned out that he was born the same time I was in the DP hospital to have my tonsils out. Now he had grown up and saved my life!

I kept in touch with Dr. Jacobowitz and Dr. Goldblatt, going in for checkups twice yearly, and we always joked around. I check Dr. Goldblatt, and he checks me. About seven years after my operation, in July 1989, I began to have chest pains again and was scheduled for an angiogram. This was my sixth hospital admission, and the test showed that two of my five bypassed arteries were once more clogged.

Dr. Jacob Shani was assigned to my case. I asked about the procedure that was planned, an angioplasty. I wondered how long it would take, and Dr. Shani explained that it's like crossing a bridge—it depends on the traffic. The length of the procedure depended on the degree of blockage.

Dr. Shani assured me that Dr. Jacobowitz would be on call in case I needed another bypass. I worried all night long and couldn't sleep. I went out to the nurses' station and asked for a pencil and paper. I went back to my room and wrote the first poem I ever wrote in my life. I wrote in Yiddish about the feelings I had, lying in bed and waiting to be operated on. I looked back on my life and forward to the future.

After the angioplasty, I continued writing Yiddish poetry, some of which was published in the *Algemeiner Journal*. Whenever I give a lecture, I ask if anyone speaks Yiddish. Once a young man raised his hand. He said he was from Johannesburg and had read my poems in South Africa. I was very proud and happy that my work was known so far away.

After the operation I was hooked up to a monitor along with another man from my neighborhood, and we were visited by a mutual friend. I went home that Friday and decided to go to shul. Doris thought I was crazy to go so soon, but I told her I had to go to thank God and see my friends.

Before I left for shul, our rabbi, who lives on the same block, came in to tell me that the other man had died an hour earlier. His funeral was scheduled for Sunday. I felt it was a miracle that I had survived and my partner on the monitor had died.

A few years later, in September 1991, I had pains in my stomach. My son recommended a Dr. Lederman, and Doris took me to see him. He checked that my heart was OK and gave me some medication in the office. I suddenly began vomiting into the doctor's sink, and was sick to my stomach for several days.

My own doctor was on vacation, and I wanted to wait until he returned, but I felt so terrible that on Saturday night I asked Doris to take me to the emergency room. We sat there for several hours without being treated or seen by a doctor, and I decided to go home. Another patient asked me how I could go home if the doctor hadn't seen me. I pointed to Heaven and said, "My doctor saw me and helped me. God helps me. I feel fine and I'm going home." We went home, but returned to the emergency room the following day.

I was in such pain I had to lean on the examining table. Doris had ordered *hallah* from the bakery, and my son Jeffrey picked it up for her and brought it to the examining room. I was lying on the table being examined by an intern. He smelled the fresh *hallah* and looked for the source of the aroma. I told Doris, "Give him a *hallah*." The intern grabbed the *hallah*, pulled off a piece and enjoyed himself as I lay there in terrible pain.

It was Rosh Hashanah eve, and nothing was done until a few days later. A doctor was assigned to me and told me that I needed a gall bladder operation. It was scheduled for Wednesday morning. Monday and Tuesday were Rosh Hashanah. Tuesday I was visited by the Bikur Holim, who blew the shofar for me. Our cantor, Nathan Glick, visited me, and so did my wife's Aunt Pearl, who lived near the hospital.

Wednesday morning I had the operation; coincidentally, the doctor put in eighteen stitches—the numerical value of *chai* (life). That was my seventh hospital admission.

The doctor asked me how many friends I have, because I had so many visitors. I went home on Erev Yom Kippur and went to shul that night. My skin was yellow, and I was weak, but I had my usual job of holding the Torah scroll during the Kol Nidre prayers and put it back into the Ark when the prayers were over. I had to enlist the help of my oldest grandson, Tracy, to hold the Torah for me because I was too weak.

I fasted on Yom Kippur as always, and when my son Tevey and his family came to our house to break the fast, my son said that I looked yellow. My catheter had started leaking. The next day the doctor removed it and I began to feel better. A few weeks later I felt as good as new when Doris and I were honored at the UJA dinner.

The eighth time was at Lenox Hill Hospital, where I had an operation on my shoulder. The rotator cuff in my shoulder was torn, and I couldn't raise my arm. The doctor put in nine stitches—half *chai*—and I was in the hospital for three days. I spent six weeks in a sling and had to sleep in a chair for that time. A woman in shul asked me if I liked to cut myself. I said, "Who wants to be cut? But if it helps, why not?"

The angioplasty was effective until March 1994, when I was admitted to Maimonides for my ninth hospital admission. I underwent another angiogram and angioplasty, performed by Dr. Jacob Shani. Before the anesthetic took effect, I asked Dr. Shani, "How is your mother?" Dr. Shani and Dr. Jacobowitz are both my friends and neighbors, and my hospital stays are more pleasant because of them.

My tenth trip to the hospital was in June. Two months after the angioplasty, I told Dr. Goldblatt that I had chest pains, and he said I should take my nitro pills. Sure enough, the nitro helped, but he made an appointment for an angiogram. I went in, and the nurses were surprised to see me again. Still, I had no choice. Dr. Shani performed the angiogram and found a sixth artery clogged. He did an angioplasty, which cleared the obstruction. I spent only one night in the hospital.

I hope never to be a patient in the hospital again. I go to my health club every day and do plenty of walking and swimming. I feel good and thank God for all the miracles He did for me. I have had the *z'chus* (merit) to help people all my life.

As detailed above, I saved my friend Joske Strugatz from drowning when we were children in Riga. In Germany, I saved a woman, Brona Ash, from drowning as well. This happened in 1946, in the city Reichenhall.

Years later, in 1959, when my family and I were vacationing in Monroe, New York, I was standing at the poolside when suddenly a teenage boy jumped into the water. He had only one leg, the result of a birth defect, and sank to the bottom of the pool. I jumped in and found him under the surface, pulled him up and pushed him over the edge of the pool. Then I walked away, because I couldn't bear to watch the lifeguard working over him. But he recovered. When I returned to check on him, he was fine and thanked me for saving his life.

In 1963, I saved a man from being killed by his own car. He had pulled his car out of the garage, which was on an incline. He had returned to the garage to close the door when the car, which he had apparently left in neutral, rolled down the incline and pinned him against the garage door. The man was trapped between the car and the garage. I heard his screams from my friend's house, where I was visiting, and ran out of the house to see who was screaming and why. All of a sudden I was Superman! I don't know where the strength came from, but I ran down the incline and pushed the car back up to the sidewalk level, releasing the trapped owner. Doris and his wife pulled him away from the car and called for an ambulance. His legs were broken, but his life was saved.

Yes, when I help others, God helps me.

15

SPEAKING ABOUT
THE HOLOCAUST

IN SPITE OF MY HEALTH PROBLEMS, I felt a holy obligation to bring
the story of the Holocaust to the widest, most diverse audience,
whether Jewish or non-Jewish. In 1983, I began to address children in classes from fourth grade through college, to allow
them to meet in person a survivor of the worst tragedy of the
twentieth century. I tell the students, "I am going to speak to
you for a few minutes about geography, biography, and history.
I guess you know what Hitler accomplished between 1933 and
1939." Then I tell them about the beginning of the war, and
what happened to the 35,000 Jews of Riga, of whom only a
minute percentage are left. I am always intrigued by the questions asked by the members of the various audiences.

Among the most frequently asked questions are queries as to
the difference between Riga ghetto and the "ghetto" of Bed-
ford-Stuyvesant in Brooklyn, New York, and requests for a
description of a typical day in Stutthof Labor Camp. My
response is that Bed-Sty is not a ghetto in the same sense that
Riga was a ghetto. I tell them that anyone is free to come into or
leave Bed-Sty at will, and its streets are open to the public,
whereas in Riga we were surrounded by triple strands of barbed

wire and guarded by armed soldiers. We were not permitted to leave the ghetto without a guard, were not permitted to walk on the sidewalks, and were under imminent threat of death.

I tell the students, "When I was the age that you guys were when you went into a high school, the Nazis put me into a ghetto. When you are of age to graduate from high school, I had 'graduated' to a concentration camp. When you were deciding to go to the prom, I was taken to the hospital with typhus."

A description of a typical day in Stutthof includes the terribly crowded sleeping quarters, the unending roll calls, the back-breaking forced labor, the almost inedible and unwholesome food, the watchtowers at the corners of the camps, the electrified wire surrounding us and the awful threat of death hanging over our heads at every moment.

My audiences are very appreciative that I come to speak with them. I feel that my appearances and work in spreading the true story of the Holocaust bear fruit. I can fulfill my obligation to make aware the widest possible audience. One teacher offered to pay me for my time; of course, I refused, and she later sent a donation to the Holocaust Museum in Washington instead. I have received hundreds of letters from students, teachers, and principals, thanking me for my visit and commiserating with the tragedies that befell me.

Speaking about the Holocaust at Flatbush Park Jewish Center

Dear Mr. Ratz—Selected excerpts from letters by educators and students

. . . we would like to thank you for the poignant lecture you gave at our Yeshiva. We greatly appreciate your taking the time to speak to our students. Your experiences during the horrifying years of the Holocaust have served as an inspiration to us all. All of our boys were deeply moved by your words and have learned a great lesson about the meaning of "mesiras nefesh." . . .

. . . we thank you for sharing your life experiences with us. Your story will be cherished and remembered by us for many years to come.

Sincerely,
Rabbi Aryeh Katzin, Dean
Sinai Academy

On behalf of the Center for Holocaust Studies, we would like to thank you for speaking about the Holocaust. . . .

The importance of speaking out publicly and creating an awareness of that which was inflicted during the Holocaust is essential for our future survival and to perpetuate the memory of those who did not survive.

We are very grateful to you for taking the time and overcoming the tremendous emotional barriers which make this a difficult experience for you. You are an inspiration to us and to all those who hear you.

Sincerely,
Prof. Yaffa Eliach, Director,
Center for Holocaust Studies

. . . your impressive presentation to our students at today's Holocaust Assembly will be always remembered.

With Rabbi Aryeh Katzin, principal of Sinai Academy

Your talent as a speaker was instantly recognized by all of us who had the privilege of hearing you.

Jack, we pray that Hashem, who spared your life from your dreadful past, will grant you a future filled with life's choicest blessings. . . .

> Sincerely,
> Naomi Benezra, Executive Director
> Crown Heights Yeshiva

Your moving and personal reminiscence as a survivor of the Holocaust genuinely touched a deep responsive chord in our students, and left an indelible impression upon them.

I sincerely want to thank you for helping Yeshiva Rambam observe the sacred memory of the six million martyrs who died al Kiddush Hashem (sanctification of the Holy Name). . . .

Sincerely,
Rabbi Chaim Medetsky
Hebrew Principal, Yeshiva Rambam

I want to extend the appreciation of my entire staff and over 500 students at [P.S.] 238 for your talk on April 16, 1985, to remember the Holocaust. I am sure that these children ages 11–15 will never forget your story, and it will live in their memories forever.

It is my hope that your experiences will help them understand the suffering of others, so that we may never again repeat the mistakes of the past.

Our hearts go out to you, and we are indebted to you for sharing your experiences with us.

Sincerely,
Lawrence Herstik
Principal, P.S. 238, Brooklyn, New York

We are deeply grateful to you for your participation in our Oral History program. We are very well aware that reawakening painful memories is a difficult and wrenching task. We know that in recording your experiences you are paying tribute to the memories of your loved ones. By entering this interview into the historical record you are acknowledging the need to teach future generations the tragic lessons of the past, so that those who died shall not have been martyred in vain.

Sincerely yours,
Yaffa Eliach, Professor
Office for Holocaust Studies

This is just to let you know that the session you led about your experiences in the Holocaust was unbelievable.

The emotions you evoked jolted us from our complacency and left impressions that will leave an indelible record.

May you and your family share many simchas.

Sincerely,
Moish Rubin
Dean of Administration
Torah Academy High School of Brooklyn

On behalf of the 8th grade magnet classes I would like to thank you for sharing your Holocaust experiences.

It was both an educational and moving experience for all. Let us hope that the memory will continue in their hearts, and that the world never experiences such horror again.

Respectfully yours,
Diane Rosen
Andres Hudde Junior High School

. . . It takes courage and stamina to bring your message to our Jewish youth day after day, year after year. May the Almighty bless you and your family with good health and the strength to carry on with your important mission.

Sincerely,
Liliane Lampert
Adm. Assistant
Taryag Academy

Thank you for taking the time to further inform us about the terrible tragedies that occurred to our nation. We really learned a lot from your experiences.

When I saw the tapes, I was on the verge of tears. The March of the Living proves that no matter what, the Nazis couldn't destroy us. The story of the ring was especially meaningful.

You are a very eloquent speaker, and you lectured with a lot of depth. I wish you the best of luck with your books. Some people, after such a terrible experience, would have crawled into a shell and not wanted to talk about it, which is understandable. Yet we are grateful that you, as a survivor, came to talk to us.

Respectfully,
Jasmin Miri Kovarsy

. . . I thought your speech was wonderful because I learned a lot about the Holocaust and concentration camps. My grandmother Mania Saks is a Holocaust survivor. She tells me things everyday. I always start crying because it's so sad. Thinking about it I do not know how you survived it's a mirical [sic].

Thanks again for telling us about your life.

Samantha Tina
P.S. 276-5-308

This letter is to thank you for your time last Thursday when you spoke about your experiences during the Holocaust. Your story helped me to visualize the Holocaust and how it was for you. For once I heard a true version not some movie producers adaptation of it. Thank you again, and we hope you can come back next year.

Sincerely,
Marc A. Masin
9th grade

. . . As I was listening to you talking I tried to put myself in your place, but I don't think I could ever feel the pain and suffering you went through. I am glad there is a memorial because people should know that racism doesn't get anywhere. It is a beautiful thing now that you are married, and there are many people that have children. The Jews will continue forever. We will keep multiplying if not for our selfs than for the people who died. Thank you for coming to our school

       Sincerely,
       Jennifer and Daniella

. . . The ring that you showed us was very interesting. I have never met a survivor of the Holocaust. The Ghetto and gas chamber sounded terrible. I hope you're leading a good life now.

       Bennett J. Fins

. . . I was one of the unfortunate students who happened to have arrived too late to benefit from your speech. I am sure, that for survivors, there are no words created yet in the human language that can ever describe the horror of the Holocaust. Therefore, I hold you in the highest respect for all your efforts in giving over your experience to the proud and spoiled generation of the nineties. I also hold you in the highest respect for surviving.

I try to learn as much as I can about that terrible period in time because I know that we must never forget. I will pass the message on to my future generations. Because of heroes like you, one day this world will be a better place. Many G-d bless you and your family and may we have the merit of seeing each other in Jerusalem next year.

       Sincerely yours,
       Yaelli Greenwald

16

THE BIGGEST MIRACLE

I SURVIVED LIBERATION by the Russian army and was cured of typhus before coming to the United States and beginning my life anew. When my family had grown, and I retired from work, I had a new dream. In 1995, I decided that I would collect money and bring it to my fellow Holocaust survivors who had remained in Riga.

I was the chairman of the board of the Flatbush Park Jewish Center, and was able to raise a substantial amount from the shul members. It was the biggest miracle of my life when I realized I would be able to help the Latvian survivors who still lived in Riga. I had already visited Riga in 1988, and had been reunited with my cousin, whom I had not seen for over forty-three years.

In 1992, I decided to return to Riga with my friends Steven and Peter Springfield, to organize the World Gathering to take place the next year, on June 11–17. We were joined by my friend Rabbi Ben Zion Pittom. The Springfield brothers went home, and Rabbi Pittom accompanied me to Israel via Moscow. We had arranged an itinerary with the travel agent such that our wives would join us in Israel.

We left Riga by Aeroflot on Monday, arrived at the local airport in Moscow, and our troubles started. The Soviet government would not allow us to leave for Israel because now that Latvia was an independent nation we needed visas to enter Moscow. The plane with our luggage on board departed for Israel, but we were stuck. The next day, we obtained our visas, but there were no flights to Israel until Thursday. We spent the time in a French hotel near the international airport; the hotel accepted only foreign money, no Russian rubles.

We finally arrived in Israel in time to hear the Clinton-Gore nomination speeches on television.

June 15, 1993, was also a very meaningful date in my life. That was when we traveled to Riga via Helsinki, to attend the World Gathering of Latvian Holocaust Survivors. Survivors came together from all over the world, meeting in Riga, at the Wall of Tears on the site of the ruins of the Gogol Street Synagogue.

We were reunited with people we hadn't seen for fifty years. I met Mr. Jaffe, a jeweler/watchmaker from Lenta. He remembered me, too. When we went on the death march from Lenta to Salaspils, we were not sure where we were going. We asked the Latvian guard if he knew our destination, and he answered, "You are going to be killed." Again, we survived by a miracle. We spent some time with the remaining Jews of Riga, distributing food and money to help them survive.

Six people with cameras recorded the historic moments. Now we had to produce a video, recording thirty hours of film and condensing it into two hours. Peter Springfield, my grandson Tracy, my friend Tony, and I were the coproducers. We made a hundred tapes for European use and a hundred tapes for American distribution, and sold them through our organization, the Jewish Survivors of Latvia, Inc. The money was distributed among the survivors in Riga. It was a big project, but we did it to help people who couldn't help themselves.

Now, on the fiftieth anniversary after our liberation, I was thrilled to be able to help the survivors who had not been as fortunate as I. They were enormously surprised that a survivor had returned to Riga to help them. In many cases, survivors return to their homeland only to visit the graves of their relatives, as I had done in 1988.

I had dreamed that I would be able to help the survivors, and they were amazed that an American citizen, who himself is a survivor, cared enough about them to bring them money and food. On one visit to Riga, I was interviewed by a Russian language newspaper, and overheard the cameraman say to his assistant, in Russian, "Look at the rich American who came to Riga."

I turned to him and said, in fluent Russian, "I live in the United States, but I'm a survivor from Riga, and I came back to see my relatives who remained here." He was stunned that a survivor had returned for practically no Jews were left from the prewar population.

I accomplished my dream of helping the survivors, and my work continues. The Jewish Survivors of Latvia, Inc., which I helped found, is still active, and even today, we are in touch with the remaining Jews of Riga. We send them money and food, and help the rabbi of the last shul in Riga to obtain prayer books and Hebrew primers.

To me, it is a miracle that my dream came true; in spite of the horrors that I suffered, I still can continue to help humanity. Since I survived, with the help of the Almighty, I feel I have an obligation to do the best I can to help other people, materially and morally. Like many others, I sent packages to Europe, specifically to Riga, so that the merchandise could be sold, and the proceeds used to support my cousin's family.

Distributing food to the Latvian survivors

A FRAGMENT FROM THE BAR MITZVAH SPEECH I GAVE ON JUNE 22, 1996
. . . As you know, today is June 22. I would like to say that you have changed June 22 from being a *Yom HaShoah* to a *Yom HaSimcha* for me. For fifty-five years, every time June 22 came around, it was a very sad day in my life because that was the date that the Germans invaded Russia and started the war.

Even the observance of my Bar Mitzvah was disturbed by the war. By that time, Jews stayed away from services because the Russian government frowned upon religious observance, and we barely had a minyan. My Bar Mitzvah was celebrated only by my being called to the Torah during the Reading. I was delighted and fortunate to bring my son to the *Kotel* for his Bar Mitzvah, and to see how he brought his own son to the *Kotel* as well, twenty-five years later.

Jeffrey's Bar Mitzvah, July 1971

Today you have made us especially proud, Moshe Yehuda Leib, Matthew Jason.

When I took my son Jeffrey to celebrate his Bar Mitzvah at the Western Wall in Jerusalem, I couldn't help but think of the time when my father took me to shul on my Bar Mitzvah, when the Russians were in control of Riga.

Similar thoughts came to my mind when my son took his own son to Jerusalem to celebrate his Bar Mitzvah twenty-five years later.

How fortunate we are to be able to practice our religion and celebrate life's milestones freely! My mind reverts back over fifty years to recall how we were repressed and forced to refrain from the practice of our holy rites by a government that imposed its will on its subjects without regard to their wishes.

| Jeffrey's son, Matthew, at his Bar Mitzvah, June 1996 | Tevey's son, Tracy, at the Kotel, at his Bar Mitzvah in the summer of 1992 |

My heart is filled with joy as I see how my family has flourished and grown with God's help. I feel that I have overcome the will of the oppressors by founding a family devoted to serving people, unlike those who wanted nothing but to destroy humanity. When Israel won the 1967 war, I decided that we would celebrate my son Jeffrey's Bar Mitzvah at the Kotel, the Western Wall of the Temple in Jerusalem.

Our first trip to Israel had been in 1969, when Tevey was eighteen, Judy sixteen, and Jeffrey eleven. We went on a three-week tour, and I was enchanted with the country. After all, it's our country, and it was at that time I made the decision to hold Jeffrey's Bar Mitzvah there.

The date was Thursday, July 15, 1971; we spent Shabbat in Jerusalem, the next Shabbat in Tel-Aviv, and the third Shabbat back in Brooklyn, where, as president of the shul, I hosted a Kiddush for all the members.

Our guests included Doris' parents, my father and step-mother, Rabbi Solomon B. Shapiro, and our friends from Israel, and the United States. Tevey spent that summer on a kibbutz, but he came to the Bar Mitzvah with a friend, and Judy's friends also joined the celebration.

I told Jeffrey, "Remember to tell your children and grand-children that you had your Bar Mitzvah at the Kotel." Twenty-five years later, Jeffrey made his own son's Bar Mitzvah at the Kotel.

I didn't have a Bar Mitzvah celebration, due to the Russian invasion of Latvia, which caused a breakdown in Jewish obser-vance all through Riga and the rest of the country. The next year, the Germans conquered Latvia, entered Riga, destroyed all the synagogues, and killed the Jews with the help of their Latvian collaborators.

Stalin and Hitler decided for the Jews that all Jewish obser-vances should stop. Despite the years of oppression, we have clean minds and healthy bodies and can follow our Jewish cus-toms and laws with impunity.

The day my mother and brother were killed, December 8, 1941, my father was beside himself, just like any other man who had lost his family. When the war ended, and we became nor-mal human beings again, he began to say Kaddish for his chil-dren and wife on the Yahrzeit, 18 Kislev, and I said Kaddish for my mother on the same day. Ironically, my father died on December 8, 1982, forty-one years to the day after my mother and brothers. (The Jewish date is 22 Kislev.)

My parents were married not quite nineteen years; my father and stepmother almost thirty-seven years. When she died on June 24, 1997, I was struck by the irony again. My older brother Mendel had been killed on the Russian front at the end of June 1942, and it may have been the same date, the 24th.

My father met my stepmother for the first time as we traveled through different countries, running from the Russian Zone in Germany, and finally decided to marry her. She was a bit skeptical about my reaction to the marriage, but I reassured her. I gave her my permission, and they were married in Munich on December 31, 1945. I couldn't be at the ceremony; I was attending the ORT school in Landsberg and living in the DP camp there.

I would go to Munich to visit my father and his wife on the weekends until I finished my ORT course. Then I lived with them in Munich for a short time until I emigrated to the United States. They joined me in Brooklyn a year and a half later, and I lived with them in the apartment I found, until my marriage on June 4, 1950.

My stepmother Dora was also a survivor. She had lived through the Warsaw Ghetto uprising, Majdanek, and Treblinka, but never spoke of her experiences. She was a good housewife, and my father had a good life with her for thirty-seven years, but after all they had experienced during the war, they both suffered very much from their nerves.

When Doris and I were married, Dora and my father led me under the *huppah*. I always wanted to be close to them, and the children and grandchildren always called her Bubby Dora. In 1971, they settled in Bat Yam, Israel, and Doris and I visited them every year. They joined us in New York for the High Holidays until my father died. Then I sent Dora a ticket to join us alone until she became too ill to travel.

The day that I left for Riga, her cousin called me to say that she was very sick. I made a detour from Riga to Israel to find out her condition. She was walking around in the hospital hallway, disoriented, sick both mentally and physically. I immediately had her discharged from the hospital and took her back to her home in Bat Yam for Shabbat. By Monday I had arranged for her to be admitted to an old age home in Holon, where she stayed for several years.

Doris and I visited her every year, and the children took their children to see Bubby Dora as well.

Our last visit was in May 1997, when we spent two weeks in Israel. Then, on June 24, in the midst of preparations for this book, I received a call that she had passed away, having almost reached the age of ninety-five. That same day, Doris and I were on the plane to Israel, arriving on the 25th of June. We intended to have the funeral that day, but the cemetery workers were on strike. I was very upset that the funeral would be delayed, and I said, "I can't wait any longer. If I have to, I'll dig the grave myself."

The funeral took place on Thursday, June 26, and I made arrangements for the monument to be erected on the following Monday. By Wednesday, Doris and I were back in the States.

My stepmother did two things for me with her passing. First, she gave me a date to commemorate my brother's death, since they died around the same date. Second, I always regretted that I couldn't say Kaddish the first year after my own mother was killed in Rumbuli Forest. Now that I am saying Kaddish for Dora, since she had no close blood relatives, I feel that I am also saying Kaddish in memory of my own mother. I thank God that I can say Kaddish for Dora, and at the same time commemorate my mother's passing.

AFTERWORD

THURSDAY, SEPTEMBER 11, 1997:
A DAY TO REMEMBER

DORIS AND I ATTENDED A BERIT that morning, celebrating the cir-
cumcision of the son of our friends, Dr. and Mrs. Abe Blank.
After the ceremony, we were ready to attend the dedication of
the new Jewish Heritage Museum in New York City. We were
fortunate enough to get a ride into the city with our good
friend Joel, and were accompanied by our friend Raya Fieg. He
had to drive a rather roundabout route in order to deliver us to
the Heritage Museum, and Raya said to him, "Why are you
going out of your way to take us to the city?"

Joel replied, "If I lived a lifetime, I couldn't do enough for
the Ratzes."

It was ironic that the dedication was held on September 11.
On that same date in 1941, my family entered the ghetto in
Riga, signaling the beginning of the end for Jewish life in
Latvia.

When we arrived at the dedication ceremony, to be held outdoors, it was raining, as if the sky was crying for the martyred
Jews, but the Battery Park City Authority had erected a tremendous covered marquee to protect the seats from the weather.

167

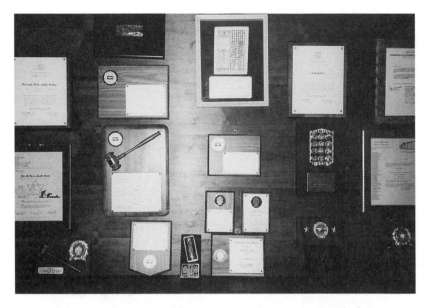

Some of the awards I received from various organizations in which I was involved.

We passed through metal detectors before entering the grounds. Miraculously, the rain stopped just as the ceremony began.

Many dignitaries were there, including Elie Wiesel, who spoke dramatically to the "passersby" who would see and enter the museum. John Cardinal O'Connor asked for forgiveness in the name of all Christians who stood by silently during the Holocaust, and even more so for those who participated in the horrors perpetrated against the Jews. Former Mayor Ed Koch spoke from the heart, even admitting that he cried as he went through the museum, which was built with his help and his far-sightedness, extending back over fifteen years.

Mike Burstyn and his mother, Lucille Lux, sang *Mein Shtetele Belz* (My Village, Belz). Their rendition was very moving, but the survivors in the audience, gently chiming in with the words, sounded like ghostly voices and brought chills to my spine and tears to my eyes.

I was very impressed although my heart cried over all the lost souls. I would have been much happier if no Holocaust museums had ever been required to exist, if all the martyred Jews could still be alive. I have a Holocaust museum in my heart; it is always with me and I am always aware of the pain of it.

In my involvement in community affairs I was happy to work with many prominent people, including Mayor Rudolph W. Giuliani

POEM

It is said that when a person faces danger, his past life flashes through his mind. This is what happened to me while I was in the hospital and I wrote the following in Yiddish.

Written by Yitzchok (Jack) Ratz, Wednesday, the 26th of July, 1989—6 a.m. till 9 a.m.—five hours before my second heart operation.

I lie in bed thinking all through the night.
I lie alone, just like a stone,
Crying endlessly,
'Why me? Why me?"
The Angel of Death calls to me,
"Come here, come here!"
I swear!
But I disappear from his sight, I swear,
And I hear his voice no longer.

As a child, I was happy and blessed, because I had my
    family,
But after my Bar Mitzvah year, the Jews' problems began.
I saw people shot, burned and hanged—

My family, as well, died to sanctify His Holy Name.

Throughout the war years
My father and I raced,
Living in need,
Because we were driven to death.

*Geshribin gevorin bei Itzchak (Jack) Ratz, Mitvuch, July 26,
1989—zex inderfree biz nine inderfree—finef shuh far mein tsvaiteh
hartz operation.*

Ich lig in bet un tracht un tracht a gantzeh nacht.
Ich lig in bet alain vee a shtain,
Un raid tsu sich alain un vain
Farvos mir, uhn a shir:
Der Malach Hamoves sugt tsu mir,
"Cum Aherr, Cum Aherr"
(Ich shver)
Uber ich farschvind fun im, Ich shverr,
Un ich herr zein shtimeh nit mehr.

Altz a kind bin Ich geven freilach un mit brucheh, Veil Ich
  hub gehat di gantzeh mishpucheh.
Nuch meine Bar Mitzvah yoren huben zich ungehoiben de
  Yiddishe tzoren,
Ich hub gezehn vee men hut geshussen, gebrent un
  gehangen,
Un aich mein mishpuchah auf Kiddush Hashem gegangen.

Mein Futter un Ich zeinen geluffen auf gich tsu existeeren
  in noit
Veil duch di milchummeh yoren hut men unz getriben
  tzum toit.

The day of our liberation became a new beginning
   for us.
We became human again, but without a home—
That caused us to cry out,
"There is no home, there is no home!"

We had no home and no family,
But one blessing remained:
Our intellect and a bit of strength.
I felt, "I need a new home."

Lo, God sent us a miracle,
He lifted His Hand and showed me a new land.

As a young man with a new wife, I began to build
A family with good fortune and blessings.
Today I am rich, with a wonderful family
And a wife who has unlimited patience for me.

My family and friends
Call me today
To find out about my health—
That creates a bond between us.

I write with a quill dipped in blood,
Trying to uplift my mood.
I go now with high hopes and patience,
Fighting for my life and survival.

I know that my hope is great,
I wish, with my family and friends,
To recover my health today.

My children and grandchildren give me joy,
Nachas and honor, which I have seen in my lifetime,
And I thank God for my dear wife He gave me.

This was all written in rhyme
In the hope that we will share much joy at a future time.

Dem tug fun unzer bafreiyung is dus gevoren far unz a
   baneiyung
Mir zenen tsurik gevoren menshen nur ohn a haim
Un dos is bei unz gevoren a gevain—
Nitoh kein haim, nitoh kein heim:

Mir huben nit kein haim un nit kein mishpuchuh—
Nor ein brucheh
Dem mayach un a bisele kayach—
Ich main, Ich darf a nayeh haim.

Ut, ut, ut—a ness hut pasirt fun Gott—
Er hut ufgehoben di hant un mir getzeikt a neyeh land.

Altz a yunger mahn mit mein froi huben mir ungehoiben
   tsu boyen
A mishpucheh, mit hatzlucheh un brucheh.
Heint tsutug bin is a gevcer mit a mispuchch ohn a shir
Un a froi mit gedult far mir.

Mein mishpuchch un freint vus
Telephoneeren mir heint
Villen visen fun mein gezundt
Un dos macht unz in a bundt

Ich shreib mit a bleifedder in bloot
Veil Ich vil ufhoben mein moot,
Ich gay yetz mit moot un gedult,
A kemfer far mein leben un tsu derleben,

Ich va:s as mein huffenung is grais—
Di vinshen fun mein mishpucheh un frient
As Ich vel gezundt veren heint.

Meine kinder un ainiklach vas geben mir fraid,
Nachas un koved vus Ich hub gezehn in mein leben,
Un a dank mein froi vus Gott hut mir gegeben.

Dus is alles geshriben mit grammen:
Alleh velen in der tzukumft huben simchas tzuzammen.

The author at one of his booksignings

The President of the Republic of Latvia and Mr. Freibergs
request the pleasure of the company of
Mr. Isak Ratz
at a Reception
on Sunday, the third of June two thousand one
at 11.30 a. m.

Regrets only: 7092106   Please bring this card with you   Residence of State President
Jūrmala, Meierovica prosp. 31

As often as I can, I journey to my birthplace. On our visit there in June 2001, the President of the Republic of Latvia received other survivors and me at a formal reception.

The author and his family at the turn of the millenia. *Top row:* Tevey Ratz, Erin Ratz, Sara Fine, Sidney Fine, Jeffrey Ratz, Pearl Ratz, Tara Ratz. *Middle Row:* Tracey Ratz, Toby Ratz, Jack Ratz, Brian Fine, Doris Ratz, Judy Fine, Matthew Ratz, *Bottom Row:* Avery Ratz, Aaron Fine, David Ratz, Elena Fine.

My two sons, Tevey and Jeffrey, with their wives, Toby and Pearl, joined my wife and myself in June 2001, as we attended memorial services at Rumboli Forest in Latvia, where my mother and brothers were killed in 1941.